CANNED PEACHES IN SYRUP

**BY
ALEX JONES**

Canned Peaches in Syrup received its World Premiere on October 6, 2007 by Furious Theatre Company, artists-in-residence at the Pasadena Playhouse. Directed by Dámaso Rodriguez.

The cast was as follows:

SCAB - NICK CERNOCH
JULIE - KATIE DAVIES
ROG (Pron: *'ROJ'*) - SHAWN LEE
BILL - ERIC PARGAC
BLIND BASTARD - DANA J. KELLY
PA - ROBERT PESCOVITZ
MA - LAURA RAYNOR
HEATHER - LIBBY WEST

PRODUCTION TEAM:
ASSISTANT DIRECTOR - MEGAN GOODCHILD
STAGE MANAGER - SUDRO BROWN
COSTUME DESIGNER - CHRISTY M. HAUPTMAN
FIGHT CHOREOGRAPHER - BRIAN DANNER
HAIR AND MAKEUP DESIGN - CHRISTA McCARTHY
LIGHTING DESIGNER - DAN JENKINS
SOUND DESIGN/ORIGINAL MUSIC - DOUG NEWELL
ASSOCIATE PRODUCER - CHRIS BLAKE
SCENIC DESIGNER - MELISSA TEOH
MARKETING & PUBLICITY - DAVID ELZER/DEMAND PR

THE SET:
(The stage is an ancient tarmaced road, which has almost been entirely engulfed by the desert, which the world is reverting to following a hundred years of drought. The whole space is covered with sand. There are a few rocks, which are broken pieces of concrete with the rusty reinforcing-steel sticking out. There is one broken concrete lamppost. There is a huge sky backdrop, which glows sourly through the veil of a stricken sky. The place is somewhere in America. The time is the future...)

ALL RIGHTS RESERVED

CAUTION: Professionals and amateurs are hereby warned that this play is subject to royalty. It is fully protected by Original Works Publishing, and the copyright laws of the United States. All rights, including professional, amateur, motion pictures, recitation, lecturing, public reading, radio broadcasting, television, and the rights of translation into foreign languages are strictly reserved.

The performance rights to this play are controlled by Original Works Publishing and royalty arrangements and licenses must be secured well in advance of presentation. PLEASE NOTE that amateur royalty fees are set upon application in accordance with your producing circumstances. When applying for a royalty quotation and license please give us the number of performances intended, dates of production, your seating capacity and admission fee. Royalties are payable with negotiation from Original Works Publishing.

Royalty of the required amount must be paid whether the play is presented for charity or gain and whether or not admission is charged. Particular emphasis is laid on the question of amateur or professional readings, permission and terms for which must be secured from Original Works Publishing through direct contact.

Copying from this book in whole or in part is strictly forbidden by law, and the right of performance is not transferable.

Whenever the play is produced the following notice must appear on all programs, printing, and advertising for the play:
"Produced by special arrangement with
Original Works Publishing."
www.originalworksonline.com

Due authorship credit must be given on all programs, printing and advertising for the play.

The Cover: Artwork courtesy of Furious Theatre Company.
Designed by Eric Pargac

All rights whatsoever in this play are strictly reserved and application for professional performance rights throughout the world and amateur performances rights outside of North America (USA, Canada and Mexico) should be made before **rehearsal** to David Higham Associates, 5-8 Lower John Street, Golden Square, London W1F 9HA. No performance may be given unless a license has been obtained.

Canned Peaches in Syrup
© Alex Jones, 2007
Trade Edition, 2013
ISBN 978-1-934962-50-3

*Also Available From
Original Works Publishing*

Terminus Americana by Matt Pelfrey

Synopsis: After barely surviving an office rampage, Mac Winchell is thrust into a nightmare landscape populated by lost Marlboro Men, psychotic vagabonds, sinister corporate thugs and a strange cult known as a "The Church of Christ, Office Shooter". Mac attempts to escape this twisted reality by undertaking a quest that ultimately leads him into the darkest corners of the American Dream. Terminus Americana is a surreal, visceral and challenging examination of our violence-saturated culture.

Cast Size: 5 Males, 3 Females, double casting

CANNED PEACHES IN SYRUP

ACT 1, SCENE 1: THE FAMILY'S CAMP.

(The family arrive on stage pulling an old wagon that has been somewhat modified.)

MA: How much further, Pa? I don't think I can manage much more.

PA: Thought I saw some green when we were on top of that last ridge, bit of grass or shrub or somethin'.

MA: Can't say I saw anythin', Pa.

PA: Could've been mistaken. *(Stops)* Wanna stop then?

MA: The girl's tuckered, Pa.

PA: You tuckered, girl?

JULIE: Bit tuckered, Pa.

PA: We'll camp up then. It's as good a spot as any: clear view all around, see anyone comin' way off.

JULIE: I'll boil some water, huh Pa?

PA: No, best not, girl; save our resources. We'll chew on them roots we dug up yesterday, plenty of moisture in them.

(They begin to make camp.)

MA: What say we put up for a few days, Pa? My legs are like jelly and my shit's ever such a funny color.

PA: What color is it?

MA: Pink.

PA: What color's your shit, girl?

JULIE: Green, Pa.

PA: That's normal then. Whatcha been eatin', Ma?

MA: That's a crazy question: the same as you of course - grass an' boiled root.

PA: Pink shit don't sound right. You could prob'ly use a rest. I just hope there's no cannibals around these parts.

MA: Don't be silly, Pa. There's no one for miles.

(Julie has set up the deck chairs and picnic table. They sit down to eat their roots.)

PA: Pink shit, huh?

MA: Bit peculiar, isn't it?

PA: Could've been that bark we had last week; that was a bit pinky underneath.

MA: But the girl's shit is fine. What about you? What colour's your shit?

PA: Green.

(Pause. They carry on eating.)

JULIE: I'm gonna have to be sick.

(Julie gets up and throws up a few paces off. The others carry on eating, regardless. Eventually she returns to the table.)

JULIE: I don't think I can manage much more.

MA: You eat up, girl - there's goodness in that root.

PA: None of us feel like eatin' that often, but we have to force ourselves. Don't let a bit of vomit put you off. You need your sustenance.

(Julie carries on eating. Pause.)

PA: We'll stay here a few days then. We've got enough provisions just now.

MA: Oh that would be nice! It's been a good while since we've had a decent break. Since the tribe broke up it seems like we hadn't stopped walkin'.

PA: We gotta find new pastures. We stay put too long, we'll starve. 'Less you fancy cannibalism?

MA: Ooh don't talk so vile! I couldn't bear the thought - meat is murder, Pa; you know that. We took the pledge with the rest of the tribe. You shouldn't even joke about it.

PA: Sorry Ma.

MA: The vegetarians are the chosen people. We'll survive because of our purity and our links with the earth,

PA: Then how come our tribe are wiped out?

MA: Oh Pa, we're still here and there are other vegetarian tribes around. It was a test of our faith.

PA: Yeah, maybe.

MA: "Flesh is weak and the grass is always greener on the other side".

PA: When we can find some.

MA: *Resolve* - that's what you're always tellin' me.

PA: Yeah, you're right Ma - *Resolve*. We'll survive.

MA: That's more like it!

(An old man with bandaged eyes, holding a wooden staff, slowly gets up from behind a boulder. Julie spots him.)

JULIE: *Pa!*

PA: *(Clocking him)* Fetch my gun, girl!

(Julie quickly gets Pa's rifle from the wagon. Pa points it at the blind man.)

PA: Who are you?

B.B: They call me *Blind Bastard.*

PA: Why?

B.B: Because I'm blind.

PA: I see. And what can we do for you, Blind Bastard?

B.B: No - what can I do for you?

PA: Well you could start by fuckin' off.

B.B: A natural reaction to a stranger in a strange land.

PA: Then naturally fuck off.

B.B: *(Walking towards Pa)* I am an old man, blind and scabby; what possible harm can I do you?

PA: Hold it right there, Mr Blind Bastard; whether you can see or not you need to know I've got a gun in my hand.

B.B: *A gun!* Do you have bullets?

PA: What use is a gun without a fuckin' bullet?

B.B: God's leaden deliverers were all spent many years ago.

PA: You can take it from me they're not all spent; one more step you can have one of your very own.

B.B: You speak through fear. But your threats are empty - you have no bullets.

PA: What's your game, stranger? We have no food to share.

B.B: Do not fear me: I am a Holy Man; I mean no harm.

MA: You're a Holy Man?

B.B: *I am the eyes of the world!*

PA: I can't see it myself.

MA: *Respect Pa.* He's a Holy Man - he has an affliction.

PA: There are plenty of blind people since the sun went crazy. It don't mean a thing. And what was he doin' hidin' behind a rock?

B.B: I sought shelter from the mid-day burn. I fell asleep... I believe you have some root. I haven't eaten for three days.

MA: Oh let him have some root, Pa - he's safe.

B.B: Thank you Madam, my blessin' upon you.

MA: He blessed us Pa. We ain't been blessed for a long time now.

(Pause.)

PA: All right, Blind Bastard; join us for a while.

B.B: Accept my scabby thanks. Please... guide me to your feast -

(Ma sits him down and hands him some root. He begins to chew.)

B.B: Very nice, very woody.

MA: It's a bit dry.

B.B: Sustenance from the soil. We must be grateful for whatever this poor maligned rock deems to give up to us. *(Chews for a while)* What tribe are you?

PA: Vegetarian: the last of the Oklahoma City Salad Men. We were nomadic; our tribe have always been grazers, movin' from pasture to pasture.

B.B: Vegetarian, huh?

MA: Are there any vegetarians around here?

B.B: Some.

PA: What tribes?

B.B: The last I saw were the Pocatello Thistlejaws and Pine-coners.

PA: What were they doin' down here? I hear there's still trees up north.

B.B: The trees are sick.

PA: We're all sick, friend. The whole world's sick, but trees are trees! A tree is a great source of protein.

MA: Would you like to try this other kind of root, Blind Bastard? It's a bit more sappy.

(Ma places another root in Blind Bastard's hand.)

B.B: You are kind, Madam. Blessin's on you and your family.

MA: Oh thank you, a blessin' never goes amiss.

PA: What other tribes have been here?

B.B: There was a group of people from the Mexico borders seen a few weeks ago.

PA: Veggies?

B.B: Meat eaters.

PA: *(Concerned)* What kind of meat?

B.B: Animal.

PA: *(Relieved)* Thank God!

B.B: There *are* cannibals 'round these parts.

PA: I knew it!

MA: Oh Pa, we haven't got to move on again have we?

PA: What's their strength?

B.B: Remnants like you: just a handful, sick and stained by the corruption of their foul misdeeds; you needn't be worried by them.

MA: Are you vegetarian then, Blind Bastard?

B.B: Of course; the only true way, Madam: redemption through earthly ties - the soil will give up its fruit once more when the canker is cut from the branch of life. The cannibals are diseased by the diseased flesh they devour. The earth will claim their bones and surrender a flower for each disgustin' corpse interred within its loamy tomb.

MA: Ooh, that's beautiful! You really are a Holy Man.

B.B: My affliction is Christ's gift; a burden and a blessin' - I can see, but can't see; the world is dark, but the way forward is bathed in light and visions. I am chosen: *Meat is murder!*

ALL: *Meat is murder!*

PA: You're welcome, Blind Bastard. I didn't know you were of our creed. Can't be sure in times like these. It's hard to trust anyone.

B.B: Think nothin' of it.

PA: These cannibals, where are they?

B.B: Some miles off. I have observed them, unseen: a crass bunch of worm-ridden carcasses, brown-drawer'd and runny-assed in the face of danger. Your gun will keep them at bay... even though you have no bullets.

PA: I have bullets.

(Pause.)

JULIE: We've got a can.

MA: Shush girl!

B.B: A can?

PA: Nothin' to speak of, just a can.

B.B: What kind of can?

JULIE: Fruit.

B.B: *A can of fruit?* I haven't seen a food can for many years.

PA: You shouldn't speak of it girl, you know that.

JULIE: But he's a Holy Man, Pa.

MA: It's an heirloom; belonged to your granpa that did.

B.B: A great treasure, no doubt. You can trust me. Let me examine it, please? I would consider it a great honor.

PA: I don't know...

MA: Oh go on. Pa. It can't do no harm.

PA: Fetch it then, girl -

(Julie enters the wagon and comes back with the can. Blind Bastard holds out his hands, expectedly. Julie passes the can to Pa, who places it in Blind Bastard's waiting hands - it is almost a religious experience. Blind Bastard begins to stroke the can. He shakes it by his ear.)

PA: Careful!

B.B: Of course... The fruit is suspended in liquid of some kind. I can feel it heavy and ripe, bumpin' against the sides of the can... What is it?

JULIE: Canned peaches in syrup.

B.B: *(Soft moan)* I know the fruit from old.

JULIE: What's it like?

B.B: You've never tasted it?

JULIE: No, it's the only can we have. I ate an apple once though; that was real nice - all crispy and wet.

B.B: Apples were fine fruit: apples and pears were prolific at one time, but a peach is somethin' much rarer.

MA: Tell us what it's like, Blind Bastard.

B.B: A peach is a soft, heavy fruit, the color of the sun; its flesh is firm and sweet to the tongue, like a small breast in the mouth.

MA: Ooh, it sounds lovely; apart from the *small breast* bit.

B.B: Why haven't you eaten them?

PA: We're savin' it for a special time when the last cannibal is dead and the land is sproutin' green again. When we know the world's on the mend, then we'll eat 'um - in celebration, like.

B.B: A worthy thought.

PA: *(Concerned for the can)* Yeah, uh can I relieve you of it, Blind Bastard? It *is* very valuable.

B.B: Of course... *(Goes to hand it over, but holds back)* But first I will bless it; it is the only can I know of. There is to my mind no other fruit upon this earth. I will pray for all of you, entrusted with this sacred object of the earth's finer time.

MA: A prayer - for us?

B.B: What are your names?

MA: I'm Ma, he's Pa, an' she's our girl, Julie.

B.B: Oh Lord God creator and destroyer, whose mighty hand once gave succour to this blighted stone! Bless Ma, Pa and Julie. Sustain them and guide them, guardians of this can of peaches in syrup. Bless this fruit oh Christ our Lord and protector. Keep it safe and free from harm, so that when the world is once again a fine and wondrous place to behold, Ma, Pa and Julie can feast in your honor upon the peach and drink the heavy sticky syrup of your love.

MA: Ooh Pa, I could cry! That was so movin'.

B.B: It is reassurin' to meet such fine people. Believe me, you will live to see this world clothed in green again.

PA: I hope you're right, friend. Sometimes I just can't see it though - it looks pretty fucked up to me.

MA: Oh Pa, it'll happen - have faith! God fucked it up to test us.

PA: No Ma, it was all the cars and chemicals that did it.

B.B: Not cars - *whales*.

PA: What the fuck's a whale?!

B.B: Great monster fish of the oceans that once swam in their millions, teemin' and spawnin' like a foul disease. Their faeces contained deadly radioactive toxins, poisonous to all but them.

MA: Who would have thought it - *whales?*

B.B: The whales were prodigious shitters. One turd could weigh as much as 300 tons.

PA: That's a big turd!

B.B: The seas began to clog with their shit - all manner of sea animal died.

PA: Why didn't people kill 'em?

B.B: They tried. Whole Cities took to sea in all manner of craft; but to no avail - all were devoured by the whales.

PA: Damn!

B.B: Finally the radioactive gas from their shit filled the sky, formin' great noxious clouds that rained their filth to the ground, poisonin' the earth.

MA: What happened to the whales?

B.B: Choked by their own shit.

MA: What... color was their shit?

B.B: What?

MA: What color was their shit?

B.B: Erm... yellow, bright yellow. Why?

MA: Nothin'.

PA: Well that is a remarkable story, Blind Bastard. I always knew it was nothin' to do with God.

B.B: God's great design can take many forms.

MA: Of course it can. God probably sent the whales, didn't he, Blind Bastard?

B.B: His punishment for all of the wickedness he saw.

PA: Well I reckon we've been punished enough.

MA: Excuse Pa, Blind Bastard. He's not really a backslider, just a bit cynical at the moment.

B.B: You must keep the faith: *Believe and the Lord will provide.*

PA: How come you haven't eaten for three days, then?

(Pause.)

B.B: *(Stands)* Christ Almighty, Lord of the apple, peach and pear..!

PA: No more blessin's, please.

B.B: I have outstayed my welcome - my apologies.

MA: Oh Pa!

PA: I don't mean no disrespect, but we've had a hard time of it lately and prayers ain't what we need just now.

B.B: Of course, I understand. I will take my leave.

(Blind Bastard stands and begins to tap his way into the desert, beyond.)

PA: Hold it right there, prophet.

(Blind Bastard freezes instantly, wincing that he has been caught. He feigns surprised innocence.)

B.B: There is disdain in your voice. What have I done to offend you?

PA: I think you've forgotten something, Holy Man.

(Pa walks up to Blind Bastard and takes the can from his hand. Blind Bastard becomes embarrassingly apologetic.)

B.B: Oh... I apologize most profusely; an aberration, a clumsy forgetful moment exacerbated by my senility and rancid old age...

MA: *(Understanding)* Anyone could have done it.

B.B: Then I will call again and share your company... if I am welcome?

MA: You're more than welcome... isn't he, Pa?

(She turns and hard stares her husband.)

MA: You're more than welcome, Blind Bastard.

(Blind bastard smiles his thanks, his brain already planning a stratagem to get the peaches.)

B.B: If you could just point me towards the ridge to the East..?

(Julie does so. Blind Bastard begins to tap his way off stage.)

MA: Will you be all right? How do you manage to find your way when you can't see?

B.B: I can see perfectly - The Lord is my guide.

(He walks straight into the side of the wagon and falls. The others help him up.)

B.B: The... ridge to the East..?

(Once again Julie points him in the right direction. As he exits...)

B.B: Bless you, benevolent strangers bound to the earth by your vegetable roots... bless you and bless your fruit; a bright glowing grail in a world fucked by flesh eating monsters - their sins will reap the whirlwind of God's terrible wrath - they will be punished!

(He taps his way off with his stick.)

PA: *(Watching)* He's fallen over again.

MA: It's marvellous how he manages though.

PA: You shouldn't have mentioned the can, girl.

JULIE: But he's a Holy Man, Pa.

PA: No matter who he is. People'd kill for that can; I've told you before.

JULIE: Sorry.

MA: Oh no harm done - he's harmless enough.

PA: I hope so.

MA: Don't be so cynical, Pa. He's a nice blind old man, totally trustworthy. When he said that prayer, it was like standin' in the rain - I felt all refreshed!

PA: *(Smiles)* Did you Ma?

MA: Yes I did - all holy and chosen.

(Pa reverently replaces the tin in a shrine on the inside door of the wagon. Ma and Julie watch.)

JULIE: Meat is murder.

ALL: *(Smiling)* Meat is murder!

(They all hug. Music as lights cross fade to and take us to...)

ACT 1, SCENE 2: THE CANNIBAL'S CAMP

(The same day. The camp is set around the rusted carcass of a burnt out car, in which they sometimes shelter. The place is littered and untidy. Scab is sitting, propped against the tireless wheel of the car. Bill is nearby, stirring the contents of a pot over a meagre fire.)

SCAB: I feel like a pile of crap.

BILL: Pretty much what you look like, Scab.

SCAB: Is it?

BILL: Yeah - all brown an' runny.

SCAB: I keep throwin' up, but I don't know where it's comin' from.

BILL: Well just stop when you see a little circle come up, 'cause that'll be your ass-ring.

SCAB: S' a joke, innit?

BILL: I think so.

SCAB: I thought it was.

(Pause as Scab looks up at the sky.)

SCAB: Look at the sun, Bill - it's like a great big red-hot ball of fire.

(Pause.)

BILL: The sun *is* a big red-hot ball of fire.

(Pause.)

SCAB: I mean it looks different.

BILL: You say that every day, Scab.

SCAB: I think it's changin' color.

BILL: Prob'ly.

SCAB: What does it mean?

BILL: Means we're all fucked, prob'ly.

SCAB: Thought so.

(Pause.)

SCAB: My skin's ever so sore, Bill.

BILL: I know, buddy.

SCAB: I could cry sometimes.

BILL: I know.

SCAB: I can't sleep for the pain.

BILL: Just keep wrapped up, Scab. Keep out of the sun; it's all you can do.

SCAB: Yeah... Think it'll clear up?

BILL: Could.

SCAB: Yeah it could, couldn't it?

BILL: Yeah, never know.

SCAB: I've seen people recover; whole body covered in crusty scabs; couldn't see their face, even.

BILL: S' possible.

SCAB: I just wish it'd rain; could do with a wash. I think if I could just wash the poison out of my body, like, it'd heal up.

BILL: Never know.

SCAB: It's real damn sore.

BILL: I know.

SCAB: It never stops.

BILL: Yeah.

(Pause.)

SCAB: How's *your* skin, Bill?

BILL: Same as always, man; bit patchy, y' know, few sun-sores here an' there. Same as everyone really; just normal.

SCAB: Hope you don't get this, Bill.

BILL: Yeah, me too.

SCAB: It's real damn sore.

BILL: I know.

SCAB: It makes me cry sometimes... the pain is terrible - like my whole body's burnin'.

BILL: These things are sent to try us, Scab... *(Spots Heather and Rog approaching)* Hey, the fellas are back from huntin'!

(Heather and Rog enter, tired and pissed off.)

BILL: How'd it go, fellas?

HEATHER: Don't ask!

BILL: But you've been gone two days. No game 'round?

ROG: Some.

BILL: What you got?

(Heather throws her rucksack on the ground and begins to unpack it.)

HEATHER: Well let's see what goodies we got in here...

(She pulls out a load of what looks like straw.)

HEATHER: Well we got us some... dry grass - *yum, yum!* An' we got us some...

(She pulls out something that looks like an old dry stick.)

HEATHER: What is that again exactly, Rog?

ROG: S' a... old dead snake.

(Heather bangs it against the car door - it retains its frozen shape.)

HEATHER: Old dead snake!

(She carries on pulling out more clumps of straw.)

HEATHER: More dry grass... and oh, you're gonna love this -

(Heather takes out a grubby sandwich box and empties out a pile of insects onto a dirty old plate by the cooking stuff.)

HEATHER: *Bugs!*

BILL: What kind?

ROG: A few cockroaches, but ants mostly - I found an old ants nest.

BILL: *(A little perplexed)* Can't go far on an ant.

ROG: What's in the pot?

BILL: Scab's vomit, boiled.

ROG: What's it taste like?

BILL: *(Tastes it)* Scab's vomit, boiled.

ROG: Any fox left?

BILL: It's head.

ROG: Let's have that then - I'm starvin'!

BILL: I was gonna save it for the weekend. I was gonna collect some of that shrubby stuff from by the brook an' boil it into a broth.

HEATHER: Never mind the gourmet stuff, Bill. We've been huntin' for two damn days! We need some grub!

ROG: How's it goin', Scab?

SCAB: The pain's terrible, Rog. Feels like my body's on fire.

ROG: You been keepin' covered up?

SCAB: Yeah. I think it would help if it rained; wash the poison out, like.

ROG: Yeah.

SCAB: Think it'll rain soon, Rog?

ROG: Gonna piss down, bud. We're in for a good storm.

SCAB: Think so?

ROG: You bet.

HEATHER: Long as it ain't like that goddamn monsoon we had two years ago; never stopped rainin' for six months!

SCAB: I wouldn't mind six months of it; wash the poison out of my system that would. S' good for the complexion, Heather.

HEATHER: You do talk crap, Scab!

BILL: He *is* crap - our very own talkin' turd!

SCAB: I *feel* like crap.

(Bill is fingering the ants on the plate, mixed with a couple of beetles and a cockroach or two.)

BILL: Y' know, I reckon these might cook up into a soup; maybe mix in some of that dry grass an' chop in the snake too.

HEATHER: Ant-fuckin'-soup - I can't wait! An' you know what, Bill; you know fuckin' what? While you're boilin' up the regurgitated remnants of Scab's stomach lining an' fricasseeing cockroaches - there are livin' people in the valley - with meat on their bones, an' livers an' kidneys an' brains an' all that lovely eatable shit that human beings are made of.

BILL: *What?!*

HEATHER: A family - three of 'em.

BILL: *Great;* let's get 'em!

(Bill gets to his feet and grabs his weapon - a samurai sword with a broken blade.)

ROG: Dunno Bill...

BILL: Come off it, Rog - pickin's is pickin's.

HEATHER: He's goin' soft!

ROG: No I'm not. Just bein' realistic.

HEATHER: We'd take 'em easy!

ROG: I'm not sure anymore. There's only the three of us now. Can't count on Scab no more.

SCAB: Sorry Rog.

ROG: S' okay Scab, not your fault.

SCAB: If it rains an' the poison's washed away, I think I'd be up to it.

ROG: Yeah, 'course you would.

BILL: We can't just let them wander off, Rog; we've got to try. There's no food left for miles. All you've brought back is some fuckin' insects!

HEATHER: He's right - when are we gonna see a decent meal again?

ROG: We need more information, Heather. Can't just go chargin' in. We'll ask Blind Bastard.

HEATHER: We saw the spasticated cunt-dick down there talkin' to them.

BILL: *Shit!* He's bound to have told them we're around here.

HEATHER: Why don't we just kill the blind fucker?

BILL: No, we can't do that, Heather.

HEATHER: Why not?

BILL: He's a Holy Man.

HEATHER: So?

BILL: It's unlucky to kill a Holy Man; you know that. Remember what happened when we killed *No Legs Cunt Face?* We lost seven of the tribe to skin cancer. Dead in less than a week - couldn't even eat them.

ROG: Yeah I remember - a mass of puss and running sores.

HEATHER: They weren't cloaked up at mid-day, it was a bad summer; the sun turned a funny color.

BILL: Yeah, but *why* was the sun a funny color?

HEATHER: It's superstition, that's all. I ain't ever gonna be suckered by those scroungin' religious pussy-rags. Listen up an' I'll give you *my* lesson for the day: eat the weak an' slaughter the crippled an' weary of the world for your own sake a-fuckin'-men!

BILL: We kill no Holy Man.

HEATHER: Bunch of fuckin' girly vaginas!

(Pause.)

SCAB: The sun's changin' color. Somethin' funny's happenin' to it.

HEATHER: Scab -

SCAB: What?

HEATHER: *Shut the fuck up!*

SCAB: Sorry.

(At that moment, Blind Bastard stumbles on stage and throws his hands into the air like Moses on acid, proclaiming his presence, making them jump.)

B.B: In the name of Saint Barack of Obama, the patron saint of terrorists an' fucked up causes, I bless this boneyard refuge and its savage tribe of Christ's dark angels - flesh for flesh!

ALL BUT HEATHER: Flesh for flesh!

HEATHER: Why do you always have to creep up on us like that, you blind asshole?

B.B: I tread with the Lord's nimble step.

(He falls over.)

HEATHER: S' funny you should turn up, you old cocksucker. I was just suggestin' we kill you.

B.B: *(Ranting, desperate)* I am a Holy Man! I am chosen! My affliction is my burden and my blessin'! It is a most pernicious sin to kill the chosen - death will most surely follow. If you recall the prophet, No Legs Cunt Face..?

ROG: Calm down, Blind Bastard. You're safe; we're not goin' to kill ya.

B.B: *(Still ranting)* Seven of your tribe dead within a week..!

HEATHER: Oh shut up you rantin' old prick!

B.B: God have mercy upon her frailty. Forgive this profanity!

ROG: We saw you in the valley, Blind Bastard.

HEATHER: With the wagon people.

(Pause.)

B.B: I have information.

ROG: That's what we want.

B.B: I must beg a favour in return.

ROG: You can have some of their meat, don'tcha worry.

HEATHER: Yeah we'll save the prick for you - you can shove it up your skinny ass; might shut you up for a while!

B.B: I deaf my ear to your verbal filth. But Christ will record every word that pours like a torrent of piss from your scummy mouth.

HEATHER: I'm gonna chew your buttocks one day, you scroungin' old cum-bucket!

ROG: Give it a rest, Heather! If we want their meat, let's get this shit figur'd out before they all fuck off... *(To Blind Bastard)* You can have a share in their flesh. Now tell us whatcha know?

B.B: There is somethin' more I want.

HEATHER: He's not havin' the fuckin' wagon - that's a damn good shelter!

B.B: Not the wagon... a can.

(Pause.)

BILL: A can?

ROG: What of - meat?

B.B: Fruit.

BILL: What kinda fruit?

B.B: Peaches.

BILL: Never heard of 'em. What they like?

B.B: They are like... fruit.

SCAB: I tasted fruit once.

BILL: What's it like, Scab?

SCAB: Nice.

ROG: I didn't know there was anythin' like that left.

HEATHER: What's so special about this can, then? Why do *you* want it so much?

B.B: It is meant for the prophet's lips alone: the Christ child Jesus himself led me to it

HEATHER: Well maybe we want the fuckin' can.

BILL: Let him have it - it's only a fuckin' can.

ROG: I've never seen a can.

BILL: S' only a scrap of metal, Rog; nothin' special.

ROG: Okay, the can's yours when we take them. So give us the low-down -

B.B: They are a family of vegetarians.

BILL: *Nice!*

HEATHER: They're dead meat!

B.B: They have a gun.

BILL: *Shit!*

ROG: Have they got bullets?

B.B: They say so.

HEATHER: They haven't got bullets. Nobody's got bullets anymore.

ROG: Did you see any?

B.B: I'm blind.

ROG: Oh - yeah.

HEATHER: I thought you were the eyes of the fuckin' world! I thought you saw everythin'?

B.B: Only what The Lord chooses to reveal to me.

HEATHER: Bullshitter!

B.B: Your words are recorded.

HEATHER: I'm gonna bake your balls some day, you blind fucker!

B.B: Your soul will writhe in hell's fires - repent now, or my curse will blight your fortunes.

HEATHER: *(Grabs blind bastard)* I've had enough of this shit!

(Bill and Rog pull her off.)

BILL: Cut it out, Heather! We can't fuck up - he *is* a Holy Man!

HEATHER: It's all bullshit, Bill! He wandered in here from nowhere, scrounges our food, an' we're stupid enough to fall for it!

BILL: You can't offend God, Heather. We can't take the risk.

HEATHER: For fuck sake, Bill - *we eat people!* Think God'd give a flyin' fuck for a cannibal?

B.B: Cannibals are the chosen people: *"The strong will inherit the earth!"* sayeth The Lord.

HEATHER: Shut him up somebody before I slice the fucker!

ROG: All right, Blind Bastard; that's enough religion for now. Anythin' else we oughta know about these veggies?

B.B: The can of peaches is an offerin' from God; it is meant for my lips...

HEATHER: *He doesn't fuckin' stop!!*

ROG: *(Shouts)* Calm down everybody!

(Pause.)

ROG: Right... We saw three - a man and two women. Any more?

B.B: They are all there is: Ma, Pa and their daughter.

ROG: Any other weapons?

B.B: I know only of the gun. When will you kill them?

HEATHER: Think we'd tell you, you withered old prick!

ROG: When we're ready. When we've reccied and got the situation figur'd.

BILL: You can fuck off now, Blind Bastard.

B.B: My gut is empty and achin'. I haven't eaten for three days.

HEATHER: Lyin' prick! We saw you eatin' with the veggies.

B.B: Dry and withered root - hardly sustenance. It is right an' proper to offer a morsel to your wanderin' priest.

ROG: Oh give him somethin' for fuck sake!

BILL: Give us your bowl, Blind Bastard -

(Blind Bastard takes a bowl from his bag and hands it to Bill, who fills it from the pot.)

B.B: What is it?

BILL: Stew.

(Blind Bastard now has to run through his well-worn priest routine before moving on - he strikes an actor's pose.)

B.B: May the hail of Mary's blessing fall like frozen rain on your coming enterprise, in the sure hope that the vegetarians die a righteous death to preserve God's hallowed race - flesh for flesh!

ALL BUT HEATHER: *Flesh for flesh!*

(*Blind Bastard exits.*)

HEATHER: *Cocksucker!*

BILL: What they look like then, these veggies?

ROG: We saw them from way off. But the girl looks tasty.

HEATHER: Yeah - nice ass.

ROG: Plenty of meat on it.

BILL: What about the gun then?

HEATHER: It's just a gun, that's all. They can't have any bullets; bullets ran out years ago.

SCAB: Yeah, but they're vegetarians remember? Nothin' to kill - they might not have used them up.

BILL: Vegetarians still kill *people* though, Scab; vegetarians kill cannibals.

SCAB: You can't blame them.

ROG: No, you can't blame them... and *we're* cannibals, ain't we? If they do got some bullets, we could die for it.

(*Pause.*)

ROG: One of us'll have to check it out.

HEATHER: Oh yeah, that's good - *"Excuse me, we're cannibals - we'd just like to know if you have any bullets for your gun?"* *"No, we just keep the gun to scare off cannibals with."* *"Great, we'll be over tonight to eat you all then."* *"All right, look forward to it - bye for now!"* Prick!

ROG: When I say one of us oughta check them out; I mean that one of us oughta make friends with them; win their confidence.

BILL: Be difficult, Rog.

HEATHER: Nobody trusts strangers anymore.

ROG: They spoke to Blind Bastard.

BILL: That's different; he's a Holy Man. Besides they didn't tell him much.

ROG: But they didn't kill him. Look boys, I agree it's desperate. I can't see us killin' anymore game for a while. I ain't seen a dog for months.

BILL: I saw a rabbit last week.

HEATHER: I'd love a rabbit!

BILL: I like 'em boiled.

HEATHER: I'd eat one fuckin' raw!

ROG: But we ain't got no rabbit, nor no dog and there's fresh prime meat out there.

HEATHER: Too right! I'm fucked if I'm gonna watch them wander off.

BILL: Who's gonna go then?

HEATHER: I'll go.

ROG: Fuck off, Heather. You're hardly the diplomatic type.

HEATHER: What the fuck's that supposed to fuckin' mean, you cock suckin' girly-vagina, turd-pusher!

BILL: No Heather, he's right. If they have got bullets, you'd take one straight off.

HEATHER: Well fuck you!

BILL: I'll go.

SCAB: No Bill..! I mean, who's gonna look after me?

HEATHER: You hear that? You fuckin' hear that?

SCAB: I only meant...

HEATHER: We're fucked to the point of starvation an' that miserable mess of diseased flesh is whining about who's gonna take care of him? Know what? It's time he was taken care of.

(Heather takes out her knife and goes for Scab.)

SCAB: *No!!*

(Bill grabs Heather.)

BILL: Leave him, you fuckin' bitch! He's one of us!

HEATHER: He's dyin', what does it matter?!

SCAB: I'm not dyin'. I just need a wash, tha's all!

HEATHER: (*Lunges again*) Kill the fucker!

(Rog and Bill scramble her to the ground. The three of them wrestle for a while. Heather is desperately trying to kill Scab.)

BILL: You're not killin' him!!

HEATHER: I fuckin' am!!

SCAB: I'm not dyin', Heather, honestly!

ROG: Grab her arm; get her knife!

HEATHER: You're all weak, piss-fuckin'-weak!

BILL: *(Now has Heather's knife)* Right - let's see who's fuckin' weak, then!

(Bill now lunges at Heather.)

ROG: *Oh fuck!*

(Rog dives on Bill, Heather dives on Rog, trying to get to Bill.)

BILL: I'll kill her! I'll fuckin' kill her! Scab is one of us!

ROG: *(Shouts)* Stop it! Stop it before someone fucks up! We've got food out there remember!!

(They all begin to calm down.)

ROG: Fuckin' shit, I don't believe you guys! You're like fuckin' animals!

(They all give up, breathless and wearied.)

ROG: I'll go, *okay?* You'd better stay and look after Scab, Bill.

SCAB: Thanks Rog. I think if it'd rain...

HEATHER: If it doesn't rain soon, Scab - how about if I piss on you?!

SCAB: If you think it might help, Heather...

HEATHER: Scabby hunk of cancer-ridden shit!

BILL: Leave him alone now - I'm warnin' yer!

ROG: Please everyone! We're the last of our tribe; we've been through a lot together, let's not forget that - *Flesh for flesh*, huh?

(Pause.)

ALL: (*Quiet*) *Flesh for flesh.*

ROG: That's better! Now let's finish the rest of that fox, and I'll slip over there first thing tomorrow.

SCAB: I'm gonna be sick!

BILL: (*Passing the pot*) In here, Scab -

(Music. Cross fade lights to...)

ACT 1, SCENE 3: THE FAMILY'S CAMP

(It is morning the following day. Pa is asleep on a deck chair outside the wagon. Ma enters from the wagon and wakes him gently. She hands him a mug of water.)

MA: Mornin' Pa. Drink of water?

PA: Oh thanks. Nothin' like water to start the day!

MA: Yes, it's nice *water* - nice and wet... All quiet then?

PA: Yeah not a soul stirrin'; couldn't hear a thing. S' funny y' know, don't even hear animals no more; birds an' night creatures an' such like - nothin'.

MA: Oh they'll come back. When the world's on the mend again.

PA: Yeah.

MA: Don't lose your faith, Pa. It's all we've got to sustain us.

PA: You don't look too good this mornin', Ma.

MA: I'm a bit worried, actually.

PA: What's wrong?

MA: It's my shit again.

PA: Still pink?

MA: Blue.

PA: *Blue?*

MA: Bright blue.

PA: *It's strange.*

MA: I know.

PA: *Blue?*

MA: Yeah.

PA: First pink an' then...

MA: Blue.

PA: *It's strange.*

MA: What does it mean?

PA: Dunno.

MA: Think its a..?

PA: What?

MA: I dunno, a... a sign or somethin'?

PA: A sign of what?

MA: I dunno.

PA: No, it's not a sign.

MA: Well what is it then?

PA: Well it's... it's...

MA: It's blue.

PA: Yeah, but it don't mean anythin'.

MA: I wish that Holy Man was here.

PA: What good would that do?

MA: He'd know what it meant.

PA: It don't mean nothin', Ma.

MA: I think it does. I think it's a symbol, or somethin' like that.

PA: A symbol of what?

MA: I don't know. Maybe God is tryin' to tell me somethin'.

PA: There's easier ways than turnin' your shit blue.

MA: You've got to admit it's not right.

PA: Well, it's not right. But it probably means you're a bit... off color.

MA: You can say that again.

PA: You need a bit of a rest up. We'll stay here a few days if we can.

MA: Thanks Pa, it would be nice.

PA: I ain't seen nothin' of them cannibals. If that blind Holy Man's tellin' the truth, we should be safe enough.

MA: I'm sure a Holy Man wouldn't lie.

PA: Yeah.

(Julie enters from the wagon.)

JULIE: I feel ever so sick!

MA: I'll chop us some root. You're prob'ly hungry.

JULIE: I don't know if I can manage any.

MA: 'Course you can. It's just what you need!

(Ma enters the wagon to get some root.)

PA: You mustn't give way to the sickness, girl. Keep eatin', that's the way!

JULIE: Are we stayin' a while then, Pa?

PA: Reckon we could all use a break. Ma's a bit peaky too.

(Ma enters with a plate of roots. They all sit down to breakfast.)

MA: *(Brightly)* Breakfast!

JULIE: I really don't feel like anythin'.

PA: Neither do I, girl. I was sick quite violently durin' the night, but I'll still force a bit of food down me.

MA: You must eat, Julie. Don't go off your food, or the sickness will get a grip.

JULIE: Okay.

PA: *(Eating, trying to encourage Julie)* Mm, this is delicious, Ma! Got a bit of flavour to it, this has.

MA: I had to dig for ages to get that. That's the very tip of the root - always the sweetest.

(Julie is staring at her plate.)

PA: Come on girl - chew up!

(Julie chews some root, half-heartedly.)

PA: That's the way! Goodness in that root; lots of fibre an' vitamins an' stuff.

MA: (*Trying to be enthusiastic too*) Mm, you're right, Pa. This really is delicious!

(They all chew for a while in silence. Eventually...)

MA: What you gonna do today then, Pa?

PA: Bit of foragin', maybe. I won't go too far; we're not desperate for provisions at the moment. I might just rest up; have a good sleep. What about you?

MA: Just have a lazy day. We hardly ever stop walkin' lately. It'll be nice to be lazy... What you gonna do, Julie?

JULIE: Don't know, Ma.

MA: What about your stones?

JULIE: Yeah.

MA: They're lovely those stones are.

JULIE: Yeah.

MA: All different colors.

PA: You're makin' some jewellery with them, aren't you girl?

JULIE: I was.

PA: I'll bet there's some colorful stones around here. Why don't you have a look around?

JULIE: No, don't think so.

MA: She's makin' ever such a pretty necklace, Pa. It's downright strikin'.

PA: Necklace, huh?

(Julie pushes her plate aside.)

JULIE: I can't eat no more.

MA: Just a bit, Julie.

PA: Try an' keep some down, girl. It's important.

JULIE: *(Getting up from the table)* I'm gonna have to lie down for a while.

MA: Try an' eat a bit more later, huh?

JULIE: Okay.

(Julie enters the wagon. Pause.)

MA: The sickness is beginnin' to get a grip on her.

PA: I know.

MA: What we gonna do?

PA: I don't know.

MA: *(Upset)* My little baby!

PA: (*Puts his arm around Ma*) There, there, Ma -

MA: I couldn't stand to lose her.

PA: We're not gonna. She's goin' through a phase I think; adolescence an' all that. She's at a funny age.

MA: But she's got to eat.

PA: Yeah.

MA: What's happenin' to us? You're losin' your faith, Julie's givin' up on life an' I'm shittin' pink an' blue! I'm goin' out of my mind with worry.

PA: *Resolve, Ma!* We'll see it through. We've had bad times before. I think this rest up will make all the difference. *(He hugs Ma.)*

MA: Oh I hope so!

(Rog enters from behind the wagon.)

ROG: Any chance of a drink of water?

(Pa instantly grabs his gun and shoulders it at Rog.)

PA: What the fuck..?!

ROG: Don't shoot me, please!

PA: Who are you?

ROG: Name's Rog - I'm a lone traveller.

PA: Bullshit!

(Julie has heard the commotion and enters from the wagon.)

PA: Keep back, girl. There might be more of them.

ROG: I'm on my own.

PA: Check behind the wagon, Ma. Be careful.

(Ma, very slowly begins to edge herself around the wagon.)

PA: What the fuck is goin' on around here? People are crawlin' from under rocks like ants!

ROG: *(To Julie)* Hello.

JULIE: Hello.

PA: Never mind the pleasantries. Just back off stranger, or you're dead an' I'm not jokin'!

ROG: You got bullets?

PA: Yes I've got fuckin' bullets! Maybe I should stick a fuckin' sign up: *"I've got bullets. Please enter if you want to be shot!"*

ROG: Can I see 'em?

PA: What's your game?

ROG: I'm just interested. I ain't never seen a bullet.

(Ma comes back from investigating behind the wagon.)

MA: No one there.

PA: I'm gonna have to shoot him.

MA: Oh dear.

JULIE: Don't Pa. Don't kill him, please?

PA: Take the girl inside, Ma.

JULIE: I'm not goin' - you can't kill him!

PA: Don't be silly, girl - he's dangerous.

ROG: I'm not. I'm just a traveller.

MA: What tribe are you from?

ROG: Vegetarian - *you're not cannibals, are you?*

MA: We are not, young man! Do we look like cannibals?

ROG: No.

MA: I should hope not.

PA: Don't listen to him - he's bullshittin'. He's a cannibal himself. One of those the Holy Man told us about.

ROG: What Holy Man?

MA: Blind Bastard.

ROG: Never heard of him.

JULIE: He's not a cannibal, Pa!

ROG: I'm not.

PA: Don't interfere, girl.

(Pause as Pa stands there, pointing the gun, ready.)

PA: *Christ...* I'm gonna have to kill him.

ROG: Please don't.

MA: Oh Pa..!

PA: Can't help it. Can't afford to risk it.

ROG: Don't kill me, please? I don't mean no harm.

PA: *(Almost crying)* I've got to kill you, you bastard! I've got a wife an' daughter here!

JULIE: Don't kill him, Pa, please? He's not a cannibal; I know it!

PA: Julie, you're all I've got. You've got to understand.

MA: He might be tellin' the truth.

ROG: I am.

JULIE: He is!

PA: *(Taking aim)* He's dead - he's gotta go -

JULIE: No!

PA: You fuckin' cannibal!

ROG: I'm not!

MA: I don't think he is.

PA: *(Psyching up to it)* You murderin' piece of shit!

JULIE: Don't do it, Pa, please?!

PA: Comin' here to carve up my family..!

ROG: I just wanted some water...

PA: My wife, my little baby..!

ROG: I'm a veggie!

JULIE: Kill him an' I'll never eat again!

PA: Don't talk silly, girl.

JULIE: I mean it: I'll never eat again - I don't care anyway!

PA: *(Tearful)* What are you doin', you bastard?!

ROG: Nothin'.

PA: What are you doin' to my family?!

MA: Let him be, Pa.

PA: I can't. You can't expect me to.

JULIE: Kill him and you kill me!

PA: Julie..?

JULIE: I mean it!

(Pa throws down the gun and collapses to the ground, weeping.)

PA: *Why can't people leave us alone?!* I don't want to kill anyone! Think I want to kill him? Think I want his blood on my hands?!

MA: *(Consoling him)* It's all right...

PA: I love you - you're my family. I can't let anyone hurt you.

MA: He's not gonna, Pa.

ROG: I'm not, honestly.

PA: Oh, give him a drink of water!

(Julie goes inside the wagon for water. Pa begins to recover from the ordeal.)

PA: Give us your story, then. Let's hear what crock of shit you've got for us -

MA: *Pa!*

PA: I'm sorry, but I just don't trust him.

MA: Give the boy a chance. You used to have such a generous nature.

PA: Yeah, that was a long time ago when the tribe was in full strength an' we all believed in somethin'.

MA: *I* still do!

(Julie enters from the wagon with a mug of water, which she hands to Rog.)

ROG: Thanks.

JULIE: S' okay.

(Rog drinks it straight off.)

ROG: *That was real good!*

JULIE: Do you want some more?

ROG: I'm all right.

JULIE: You can have some.

ROG: I won't just now, but thanks.

JULIE: S' okay.

ROG: I appreciate it.

JULIE: Thanks.

ROG: S' okay.

JULIE: What's your name?

ROG: Roger, but... you can call me Rog. What's yours?

JULIE: Julie.

ROG: That's a nice name.

(Pa has been watching this exchange, gob-smacked.)

PA: Excuse me, *Rog* - I hate to interrupt you when you seem to be gettin' on so well with my daughter, but if you don't mind my askin' I'd be quite interested to know just where the fuck you came from an' what you're after?

ROG: I'm not after anythin'.

PA: *(Incredulous) A lone traveller?*

ROG: My friends were ambushed.

PA: Oh yeah?

ROG: By cannibals.

PA: Bullshit!

MA: Pa!

JULIE: Maybe it's the tribe the Holy Man told us about.

MA: Near here?

ROG: No, about three days away. Are there cannibals around here?

MA: Only a few.

JULIE: Nothin' to worry about.

ROG: *Thank God!*

PA: What happened to your friends?

ROG: What do you think?

MA: God bless their bones!

PA: Three days without water?!

ROG: I had some water. I drank it.

PA: He's a fraud.

JULIE: He's tellin' the truth.

PA: How do you know?

ROG: I am.

JULIE: I just do. I can feel it.

PA: You're not makin' sense, girl. You can't trust a stranger.

MA: He's got a nice face.

ROG: Thank you.

MA: That's all right.

PA: A nice face?

JULIE: He has.

PA: What does that prove?

MA: Well... that he's... all right.

PA: Oh I give up - what's the point?!

JULIE: Can he stay with us, Pa?

PA: No!

MA: Oh Julie, you don't even know that he wants to.

ROG: I could use the company.

PA: We're a family, stranger. We travel as a family.

MA: Oh Pa, he's alone - he lost his friends.

PA: So he says.

ROG: I did.

PA: We can't just take in a complete stranger. Besides, we don't have enough food.

ROG: I'm a good forager.

MA: There you are!

ROG: And I'd be a handy fist against any cannibals.

PA: Thought that's who you were runnin' from.

ROG: We were ambushed.

JULIE: They were ambushed, Pa.

ROG: I finished one off.

PA: Don't bullshit me, boy.

ROG: I did.

JULIE: He did!

MA: Be nice to have a bit more protection.

PA: I don't know...

JULIE: I get ever so scared sometimes. There's only the three of us.

PA: I take care of you, girl.

MA: You're not gettin' any younger, Pa.

PA: Thank you!

MA: Be nice to have someone around, 'till we meet up with a decent sized tribe.

PA: If there are any decent sized tribes left.

MA: Pa is goin' through a bit of a doubtin' period. Are you religious, Rog?

ROG: I am, as it happens.

MA: The vegetarians are the chosen people.

ROG: I know.

MA: Salvation through our links with the earth.

ROG: Meat is murder.

ALL BUT PA: Meat is murder!

PA: Oh all right, all fuckin' right! He can stay, but just for a while, 'till he's rested an' recovered. I'll be keepin' an eye on you, boy. If you fuck up once, you're out. An' I don't care either way if you believe me, but I can assure you there *are* bullets in this gun; just bear that in mind.

JULIE: Oh Pa, how could you say such a thing?!

ROG: No Julie, Pa's right. Why should you trust a stranger? These are sad, desperate times we live in. And it's so rare to come across a real family - a family that cares for each other. Pa, I don't blame you for bein' suspicious of me. If I were in your shoes I'd feel exactly the same; so if you don't want me around, just tell me and I'll leave.

JULIE: No!

ROG: Yes - it's only right. But I swear, Pa; give me a chance an' I'll prove myself to you. I can provide, be useful, pull your wagon.

PA: You're not sleepin' in it.

MA: There really isn't room.

ROG: I wouldn't presume.

JULIE: You will stay, Rog?

ROG: I would consider it an honor an' a privilege to spend some time with y' all. But only if Pa wants me to.

(Pause. They all look to Pa.)

PA: *(Sighs)* Give the boy some root, Ma.

JULIE: Oh thank you, Pa!

(Julie fetches another chair and they all sit down together at the table.)

PA: If you're joinin' us, boy, you'll have to prove yourself. After you've eaten, have a rest an' then go out foragin'. We'll see if you're worth the trouble.

JULIE: Oh Pa, not in the mid-day burn!

PA: He can cloak up.

MA: That's a bit much to ask.

PA: If he wants to stay he won't mind.

ROG: *(Chewing)* I don't mind.

JULIE: You must keep yourself covered, Rog.

ROG: I will.

MA: There was a boy in our old tribe who got caught in the open without protection - baked in his own skin, he was.

ROG: I'll keep covered.

PA: You'll be all right if you're covered. You can take a bottle of water with you.

ROG: Thanks.

PA: *(Rising)* I've been up all night lookin' out for *cannibals*. So if you'll excuse me, I'll just get my head down for a while.

ROG: Thanks for takin' me in, Pa.

PA: I haven't taken you in. You're under surveillance, boy. If you're okay... well, *okay*.

ROG: I will be.

PA: I sleep with my gun, by the way.

(Pa enters the wagon.)

MA: *(Squirming a little)* I'm gonna have to go myself... *(Rises)* Rog, what color's your shit?

ROG: Erm... normal color.

MA: Oh... *must go* -

(Ma exits behind the wagon.)

JULIE: Don't mind Pa - he's just bein' protective.

ROG: I don't blame him. He's got a beautiful daughter.

JULIE: *Beautiful?*

ROG: You are.

(Pause.)

JULIE: (*Smiles*) I've never been called beautiful before.

ROG: I ain't never called anyone beautiful.

JULIE: I don't like to think of you foragin' in the heat of the day... I could do some searchin' on the opposite side of the ridge; put what we find together. Pa'll never know.

ROG: My conscience wouldn't allow that, Julie. You're too frail for that kind of labor. I'll forage gladly, knowin' that any food I bring will find its way to your lips.

JULIE: I've never seen anyone like you before.

ROG: I've never met anyone like you.

JULIE: Your eyes are weird.

ROG: Thank you... I really like your hair.

JULIE: I washed it last year.

ROG: It's cool.

(Pause.)

JULIE: We've got a can.

ROG: Yeah?

JULIE: Yeah - a can of peaches. They're like small breasts.

ROG: Sounds nice.

JULIE: I'm glad you're stayin'.

ROG: Me too.

JULIE: You've got *weird* eyes.

ROG: You've got nice tits.

JULIE: Thank you.

ROG: Can I touch 'em?

JULIE: *Ooh - yes please!*

(Julie quickly unbuttons her shirt and lets Rog fondle her breasts.)

ROG: *(Feeling her tits)* They're real nice...

(It's all too much for them and they suddenly find themselves in each other's arms, desperately smothering each other in kisses. After a long and passionate embrace, Julie breaks away.)

JULIE: I'm gonna have to be sick.

ROG: Oh right. See you later.

JULIE: See you, Rog.

(Julie exits behind the wagon. Rog is staring out in front of him, a look of pure wonder on his face. Music begins to play. A short pause as the music begins to establish itself.)

ROG: *(Through the music)* I can't eat her! She's beautiful..! Christ - *she's beautiful!*

(As the music progresses and builds, a wonderful smile begins to grow on Rog's face. As the slow, quiet opening reaches its small crescendo, the smile suddenly becomes a beaming grin. The lights fade to blackout as the music builds to a climax.)

END OF ACT I.

ACT 2, SCENE 1: THE CANNIBAL'S CAMP

(A few days later. It is the afternoon. Scab is alone, sleeping. He is wrapped up in a heap of rags. Heather enters carrying a dead hedgehog. She kicks Scab.)

HEATHER: You dead yet?

SCAB: *(Waking)* Oh hello, Heather. What you got there?

HEATHER: A hedgehog.

SCAB: *A hedgehog?!* Perfect - Bill loves hedgehog!

HEATHER: Where is the lazy cunt?

SCAB: Gone to the brook for some water. Said he'd have a wander around; see if he can see any sign of Rog.

HEATHER: Huh - what a fucked up plan that was! Should've just gone down there an' slaughtered the fuckers straight off.

SCAB: You think they killed him?

HEATHER: It's the downright waste of a good life that gets me - fresh meat an' they won't even eat the sorry-assed fucker.

(Pause. Heather settles down by the campfire.)

SCAB: Will you eat me when I croak?

HEATHER: Yep - 'fraid so.

SCAB: Maybe... you could, I dunno... bury my bones?

HEATHER: Gonna boil them up for soup. But tell you what, Scab, after I've chewed you all up, I'll have me a good shit an' say a prayer over it - how's that sound?

SCAB: It's something, I guess.

(Bill enters with gas cans full of water strapped to his back.)

HEATHER: Hey cunt-dick!

BILL: How you doin', bitch-face?

HEATHER: Better than you - you look like shit.

(Bill wearily unstraps the gas cans.)

BILL: Bit worried - the brook's turned a funny color.

HEATHER: It's always been a funny color.

BILL: It's funnier.

HEATHER: Why aren't you laughin' then?

BILL: *(Ironic)* Ha, ha, ha!

SCAB: Think it's safe?

BILL: Dunno. It's gone all murky... an' it smells.

HEATHER: If the sun don't get us the water will, huh?

BILL: It's gettin' lower too - isn't much more than a puddle.

HEATHER: Well ain't life just fuckin' wonderful!

SCAB: We can't live without water.

HEATHER: We're gonna have to move on; find a better supply.

BILL: It took us three months to find this one.

HEATHER: Yeah.

BILL: What about Scab?

HEATHER: Fuck Scab, Scab's fucked!

BILL: I'm not leavin' Scab behind.

SCAB: Thanks Bill.

HEATHER: Who said anythin' about leavin' him behind?

BILL: Be difficult to carry him.

HEATHER: Not if he's sliced up proper.

SCAB: Don't finish me off, fellas? I mean you never know; I might get better.

BILL: No one's goin' to slice you, Scab, don't worry.

HEATHER: The meat's rottin' on his fuckin bones! There won't be anythin' left to pick at soon.

BILL: Leave him alone, Heather, for Christ sake.

(Pause as Bill pours some water from the can into a mug and passes it to Scab.)

SCAB: Heather's got a hedgehog, Bill.

BILL: A hedgehog?!

HEATHER: (*Holding it up*) Couldn't believe my eyes. Just scuttled out from behind some shrub. Curled up all convenient like as soon as it saw me.

BILL: I love hedgehog!

HEATHER: Won't go far.

BILL: Further than fuckin' ants.

HEATHER: No sign of Rog then, huh?

BILL: No.

HEATHER: Been gone two days. They must've killed him.

BILL: Stands a chance. Shit, there'll only be three of us left!

HEATHER: Two an' a turd - Scab don't count.

SCAB: Sorry.

HEATHER: S' all right, turd.

(Blind Bastard enters.)

B.B: Behold - the servant of The Lord is cometh to receive the fruits of his righteous labor!

HEATHER: Oh fuck, here comes the scroungin' preacher!

B.B: I pardon your profanity.

HEATHER: We've got nothin' for you - *fuck off!*

B.B: I turn my cheek to your insults, in the sure knowledge that your purulent flesh will roast for eternity in hell's kitchen.

BILL: What do you want, Blind Bastard?

B.B: I have come to claim my reward for information tendered: the can of fruit that The Lord revealed to my eyes.

HEATHER: *What fuckin' eyes?!*

B.B: I am the eyes of the world.

HEATHER: No - you are the prick of the world!

B.B: I will pray for you.

HEATHER: Don't waste your breath, cunt-rag!

BILL: Rog isn't back.

B.B: Do not seek to cloud my way with diuretic phrases. I recognise your deception and demand my fruit.

HEATHER: What's he talkin' about?

B.B: You have my peaches!

BILL: No honestly, Blind Bastard, he hasn't come back.

B.B: Christ in his majesty will infest your body with terrible cancers if you deceive me.

HEATHER: Let's kill him. Bill -

BILL: No Heather, it's unlucky.

B.B: The peaches are mine. The Lord himself led me to 'em. They are the prophet's fruit; should anyone else partake of their flesh, they will sin in God's eyes and forgo their place in Paradise.

BILL: We haven't got them, Blind Bastard. Rog hasn't come back. They must've figur'd him out an' killed him.

(Pause.)

B.B: The peaches are promised me...

(Heather suddenly grabs Blind Bastard by the throat.)

HEATHER: It's time to die, socket-face!

BILL: *Oh not again!*

(Bill pulls her off.)

BILL: For Christ sake, Heather, leave him be!

HEATHER: Well tell him to fuck off then. 'Cause if he hangs around here any longer, complainin' an' fuckin' whinin', he can kiss his ass goodbye!

B.B: I curse your rancid soul, you foul-smellin' piss-mouthed harridan!

(Heather draws her knife. But Bill grabs her yet again.)

HEATHER: I want to kill him! Why can't I kill the bastard?!!

BILL: *(Holding her back)* He's a Holy Man; you know it!

B.B: May Christ's curses fester and grow like a disease up your mouldy crack - *you are damned!!*

(Heather breaks free of Bill and dives at Blind Bastard, grabbing his legs. He falls over, but Bill is quickly there, struggling in the muddled heap to hold Heather down.)

HEATHER: *That is it, asshole!* I'm gonna be carvin' you up tonight!!

B.B: Lord deliver me from this monster!

BILL: Get away, Blind Bastard while you can!

(Blind Bastard scrambles up while Bill is struggling with Heather, but falls on top of Scab.)

SCAB: (*Screams in pain*) *Aaghhrrr!!* Oh fuck!! Please, please get off me! You're burstin' all my blisters!!

HEATHER: Bleed on him, Scab! Give him a disease!

B.B: *(Getting up)* I will search out the can myself!

SCAB: *Oh the pain!*

B.B: *(Staggering off)* I will seek out this grail and command the vegetarians to surrender its holy power to me!

SCAB: *Oh, it's painful!*

HEATHER: *(Warning)* Next time, preacher!

B.B: *(Almost off)* I curse your soul, you rancid, foul-smelling skank-bitch!

(Blind Bastard falls over, gets up and staggers off stage. Bill releases Heather.)

HEATHER: What is wrong with you, Bill? Enough is e-fuckin'-nough! He's goin' fuckin' nuts. His brain's turnin' into a peach!

BILL: We can't risk killin' him! We might bring God's curse down on us.

HEATHER: *(Weary)* Oh bullshit! You are a dickhead, Bill. You're a dickhead, an' that cocksucker *(Indicating Scab)* is an asshole!

SCAB: I'm fuckin' bleedin'...

HEATHER: You're *fuckin' pathetic!* I'm gonna find some clay to bake this little fucker in... Or should I boil it?

BILL: Clay's best; fetches its spines off when you crack it open.

HEATHER: *(Exiting)* Ah well, at least we'll eat somethin' tonight.

BILL: Thanks Heather.

HEATHER: Fuckin' lesbian ho-bag slut!

BILL: You're a treasure.

HEATHER: *Lesbian!*

(Heather exits.)

BILL: You bleedin' much?

SCAB: I don't know... He just burst a few blisters, I think. But I can't bear anybody touchin' me. It even hurts when I lie down.

BILL: You don't look too good, Scab.

SCAB: I'm sick of the pain, Bill. I mean it never stops - it's like the whole of my body's on fire. It's real damn scary... I don't want to die; I don't know why - there's not much to miss, really: we're always uncomfortable, we're always sufferin'. But it's still life, I s'pose - it's still experience.

(Pause.)

SCAB: I never really enjoyed eatin' people, y' know; I never really approved... When I think of all the people we killed... *Christ - little children, too!*

BILL: It was us or them, Scab. S' called survival.

SCAB: It's horrible though, isn't it?

BILL: I never really knew any different. I was brought up as a cannibal; all my family were cannibals. I even ate *them* when they croaked.

SCAB: Yeah... Thanks for bein' my friend, Bill.

BILL: S' okay, Scab.

SCAB: I... I love you, y' know.

(Pause.)

BILL: I love you, Scab.

SCAB: You're like a father to me.

BILL: Fuck off, Scab - you're older than me.

SCAB: A brother I mean, I think. I mean I never really had any family so, y' know I don't really know how it all works... But anyway, if I did have family, I wish you'd been it.

BILL: We *are* family.

SCAB: *(Begins to cry)* I don't want to die, Bill, I don't want to die. But I am, I'm goin' to soon, ain't I?

BILL: Yeah... you are.

SCAB: I hate the pain; but the thought of not ever feelin' anythin' again...

BILL: It'll be a release when it comes man, honestly.

SCAB: Y' reckon?

BILL: You'll want it when it happens, Scab - it's natural an' right.

SCAB: Hold me, Bill.

BILL: What?

SCAB: Hold me, please?

BILL: All right. Come here, you big softy.

(Bill embraces Scab.)

SCAB: That's real nice.

BILL: Yeah.

SCAB: Nobody's ever held me before.

BILL: People don't bother much nowadays.

SCAB: I always wanted it - to be held, to be cherished.

BILL: *(Laughs)* Hold on there, buddy!

SCAB: S' like a dream come true.

BILL: You sure do stink, Scab!

SCAB: I love you, Bill.

BILL: Yeah.

(Music. Cross fade lights to...)

ACT 2, SCENE 2: THE FAMILY'S CAMP

(Early evening, the dusk is just about to give way to night. The sky gradually darkens throughout the scene to reveal a night sky spangled with stars. Rog and Julie are sitting together on top of the wagon. Rog's arms are around her.)

ROG: I didn't believe this could happen.

JULIE: Me either.

ROG: All of a sudden there's a future, a purpose.

JULIE: It's ever so excitin'.

ROG: I love your straggly hair.

JULIE: You're so weird. Your eyes are peculiar.

ROG: These eyes have seen a lot.

JULIE: Maybe that's why.

ROG: You know what I think?

JULIE: What?

ROG: I think things'll get better. I've got a strange feelin' that we're over the worst of it. Y' know some people reckon that it's all there underground, waitin' for the right signal to start up again; seeds an' stuff buried deep an' snug.

JULIE: D'yer really think so?

ROG: One day it'll all shoot up. There'll be trees an' bushes an' plants an' clean water...

JULIE: And money.

ROG: What's money?

JULIE: *Money's wonderful!*

ROG: I never heard of it.

JULIE: Pa told me about it. He's always tellin' me history stories about how the world use to be. I mean it's always been crackin' up, like, but there was more people an' green stuff an' all sorts of crazily shaped animals, an' there was stores where you could buy food with money.

ROG: So what is it?

JULIE: Bits of metal an' paper. You could swap 'em for food.

ROG: I don't believe that!

JULIE: Pa says so.

ROG: Why would anyone swap food for a bit of paper?

JULIE: Dunno, but they did.

ROG: It must have been cool. I hope money comes back.

JULIE: It will.

ROG: Yeah I think it will. You an' I will see a new age dawn - you just wait!

JULIE: You won't ever go away, will you Rog?

ROG: Never. I want to spend the rest of my life with you.

JULIE: This past week has been like a spectacular dream. I'm scared I might wake up and you'll disappear.

ROG: I'll never go.

JULIE: I couldn't live without you. You make me feel great - I've only thrown up twice today.

ROG: *Oh Julie!*

JULIE: I love you, you weird bastard!

ROG: I love you: I want to pick your scabs and bathe your sun-sores with rainwater. I want to stroke your filthy thighs and screw you under the twinklin' stars.

JULIE: You say such wonderful things!

ROG: I mean 'em. I love you. I want to fuck you.

(Julie spots her parents approaching.)

JULIE: *(Excited)* Oh, can I tell Ma an' Pa?

ROG: I think you'd better.

(They kiss.)

ROG: I'll wait for you at that outcrop.

JULIE: *Oh Rog! You're gonna fuck me!*

ROG: I'll be waitin'.

(Rog exits as Ma and Pa wander on. Julie jumps down from the wagon.)

MA: We're not disturbin' anythin', are we? Where's Rog gone?

JULIE: He's waitin' for me at the outcrop behind the wagon.

MA: What for?

(Pause.)

JULIE: (*Delighted*) He said he wants to fuck me!

(Ma embraces her daughter, delighted too.)

MA: *Awww!*

PA: Fuckin's all fine an' well, but what about your future? It's a provider you need, a good forager, not sex.

MA: Aah, there's not many'd bother nowadays though, Pa. I can't remember the last time we had a fuck.

PA: We have a daughter. It must have been then.

MA: Yes, but to want to *fuck her* - he must love her.

PA: An' what about you? Do you want to fuck him?

JULIE: Yes I do!

MA: Listen to her. She's no idea what fuckin's about.

JULIE: Yes I have.

PA: Won't last. There's not many can manage it now.

MA: But maybe it's love that does it, spurs you on, beats the sickness.

PA: *(Laughs)* I can't see it myself! Look if you want to try your hand at fuckin', you go ahead. But don't be disappointed, 'cause I doubt whether much will happen.

JULIE: Oh it will!

(Ma and Pa laugh.)

MA: *(Sudden thought)* Oh, what if she gets taken with child?

PA: It's not possible anymore, is it?

MA: I don't know.

PA: Somethin' in the water, I think; acid in the rain.

MA: She might.

PA: When was the last time you saw a baby?

(Pause.)

JULIE: So can I have a fuck, then?

PA: If you can manage it, you go ahead. You enjoy yourself, girl!

JULIE: *(Excited)* Thanks Ma, thanks Pa!

(She runs off to Rog.)

MA: I'd never have thought I'd see her fuckin'.

PA: She's growin' up.

MA: I haven't seen her so well for ages. She's definitely eatin' more.

PA: There's somethin' odd about that boy, mind... Still, if he can make my baby happy, who cares?

(Pa puts his arm around Ma.)

PA: Remember when we first met?

MA: Inter-tribal dance: *Salad Men and The Muskogee Grazers.*

PA: Those were the days! All those people...

(Pause.)

PA: An' how are you now, Ma?

MA: Well -

PA: Your shit again?

MA: Orange.

PA: Orange now?

MA: Yeah - orange.

PA: You haven't..?

MA: What?

PA: Well... you haven't tried... tastin' it?

(Pause.)

MA: Think I should?

PA: Dunno.

MA: I hadn't thought of tastin' it.

PA: Might be an idea.

MA: I'll give it a go.

PA: Might give us a clue as to what it is.

MA: Never thought of tastin' it.

PA: Might be an idea.

(Pause as Pa looks up at the night sky. The sky is now awash with stars.)

PA: Look at those stars, Ma - millions an' millions of 'em twinklin' away like sparks from a gigantic bonfire. This is when I really feel alive; standin' under all this - it's all so immense an' wonderful. We're just a tiny part of some crazy accident; a little blue speck of life in space that 'll soon go out... They had machines y' know that could fly through space. People have walked on other worlds where no person had ever been: great big empty planets where nothin' could live, nothin' could breathe. Pretty soon this world will be just another empty planet, spinnin' its lonely journey through space... *fuckin' whales!*

MA: God must have had a good reason for sendin' them.

PA: *If* God sent them.

MA: I wish you'd let God back into your heart. I wish you'd believe again.

PA: I still believe in the vegetarian creed: meat is murder.

MA: *(Obediently)* Meat is murder.

PA: But I find it difficult to find sympathy with a God who would fuck everythin' up just to teach our ancestors a lesson.

MA: I'll pray for you.

PA: *(Smiles)* Thanks Ma. Let's get some shuteye, huh?

(Ma smiles back and enters the wagon. Pa sits in his deck-chair with his gun and looks up at the stars.)

PA: Is there anyone out there?

(Pause.)

PA: Didn't think so.

(Music. Lights fade to black out.)

ACT 2, SCENE 3: THE FAMILY'S CAMP

(The next morning. Rog is sitting in Pa's deckchair. There are a few wispy clouds in the sky. Julie enters from the wagon. She smiles.)

JULIE: Where's Pa?

ROG: He's gone to scout for water. If he don't find any he said you'll have to be movin' on soon - search out a safe haven somewhere.

JULIE: Oh...

ROG: I asked him again if I could come along - he said yeah.

(Julie leaps at Rog, hugging and kissing him.)

JULIE: *Oh Rog, Rog! You're comin' with us!*

ROG: *(Laughing)* I know!

JULIE: We can fuck lots more.

ROG: You bet!

JULIE: It was amazing!

ROG: I know!

JULIE: I really like it.

ROG: Me too... Guess what?

JULIE: What?

ROG: There was rain last night.

JULIE: *Rain?!*

ROG: Look at the sky -

JULIE: It looks different.

ROG: Clouds.

JULIE: Yeah - *clouds*.

ROG: An' it looks bluish.

JULIE: Yeah, yeah it does.

ROG: Look -

(Rog hands Julie a flower he has concealed.)

JULIE: *A flower!*

ROG: Yeah.

JULIE: A flower.

ROG: A flower.

JULIE: It's beautiful.

ROG: I picked it for you.

JULIE: Thank you.

ROG: *(Smiles)* It's a sign, a beginnin'.

JULIE: It's been a while since I've seen one.

ROG: I know.

(Ma enters from the wagon.)

JULIE: Look Ma -

MA: *A flower!*

JULIE: I can't remember when we last saw one.

MA: We ate some last year.

JULIE: Not as pretty as this.

MA: *(Smiles)* No, not as pretty as that.

ROG: It rained last night.

JULIE: Look at the sky, Ma -

MA: *(Smiles)* It looks good. Been a long time since I seen clouds like that.

JULIE: There'll be more; I know it.

MA: Maybe there will.

JULIE: Just look at those clouds!

ROG: There's still seeds in the earth, y' know.

MA: Do you think there are?

ROG: Yeah, just waitin' for the right signal to start up again: new growth, tiny green shoots of life, snug an' warm.

MA: It does look different.

JULIE: He gave me a flower! Nobody's given me a flower before.

MA: Where did you find it?

ROG: About half a mile away, near an old car skeleton.

JULIE: Pa's lookin' for water, let's go find him, Ma. - show him the flower.

MA: Maybe there's some more.

ROG: There might be.

JULIE: Please Ma, it's a new beginnin' - let's tell Pa!

MA: We could look for some more flowers...

(Julie exits, Ma follows, but stops and turns to Rog.)

MA: I just wondered, Rog...?

ROG: Yeah?

MA: Do you know anythin' about yellow shit?

ROG: Yellow shit?

MA: Does it mean anythin'?

ROG: I... don't think so.

MA: The whales shit yellow, didn't they?

ROG: What's a whale?

MA: It doesn't matter.

(Julie comes back to hurry her mother along.)

JULIE: Come on, Ma!

ROG: You go on. I'll keep watch.

MA: Thanks Rog - you're a good boy.

JULIE: He's definitely comin' with us when we move on.

MA: *Oh I am pleased!*

(They begin to exit again. Suddenly Julie runs back and pulls a filthy ribbon from her hair. She hands it to Rog.)

JULIE: You gave me a flower. I want to give you somethin'.

(Julie runs off after Ma, who has already exited.)

JULIE: *Fuckin' is fantastic, Ma..!*

(Rog is alone. There is a pause as he looks at the ribbon.)

ROG: A flower... I picked a flower this mornin' for my love. *(Laughs)* There must be a right fucked up star out there somewhere winkin' its light at me! Life is beginnin' again - it's a miracle. *Oh Julie!*

(Rog kisses the ribbon in his hand, making a vocal sound of it. Blind Bastard rises from behind a rock.)

B.B: And Judas betrayed the Lord with a kiss!

ROG: Blind Bastard!

B.B: We had given you up for worm food, cannibal.

ROG: Don't call me cannibal.

B.B: I have been listenin' with interest to your conversion. No doubt Bill and Heather will find this sudden change of heart a little surprisin', too.

ROG: Don't give me away, Blind Bastard.

B.B: You promised me the can.

ROG: The situation has changed.

B.B: You have broken a holy vow!

ROG: These are decent, honest an' truthful people. I feel at home here.

B.B: They are vegetarians.

ROG: And so am I now.

(Pause.)

B.B: Deliver the can to me before the end of day, or your secret will be revealed.

ROG: You bastard!

B.B: *Blind* bastard!

ROG: I could kill you now.

B.B: How would you explain my corpse to your friends?

ROG: I can't get the can - I can't.

B.B: You will find a way.

ROG: You're no religious man. You're just a fuckin' opportunist! Heather was right - it's all a big pretence, isn't it? Why are all Holy Men cripples and deformed outcasts?

B.B: We bear Christ's sufferin'. We walk in silent agony.

ROG: There's nothin' silent about you, you malicious connivin' cunt!

B.B: Your slanders are of no consequence. I desire the can. Bring it tonight to the camp.

ROG: So Heather can slit my throat?

B.B: So I can receive it in safety... I hear your friends approachin'. I suggest you take a walk. Any communication between us might hint at some previous familiarity.

(Rog grabs Blind Bastard and holds his knife to his throat.)

ROG: You're an evil piece of shit! You'd better watch your back... Oh, but you can't, can you? You're blind.

(Rog releases Blind Bastard and exits. A short pause and Julie enters, holding a few flowers, followed by Ma and Pa.)

JULIE: *(Entering)* We've found some more flowers, Rog..! Oh - Mr. Blind Bastard!

B.B: God bless this dusty haven!

MA: It's the Holy Man!

JULIE: Where's Rog?

PA: Where's the boy?

B.B: I thought there were only three of you.

MA: There are... *were*. A traveller joined us recently.

B.B: Then he is fortunate to have found such friendly people to fall in with.

JULIE: He fucked me.

B.B: May his seed bear you sweet fruit.

JULIE: He's got a seed?!

MA: He means, *"May he give you a baby"*.

JULIE: A baby?!

PA: You won't have a baby, girl.

JULIE: But he just said...

PA: Never mind what he said. Nobody can have babies anymore.

B.B: Faith can fire the faintest subterranean stirrin's to life: the womb is a holy temple.

PA: The womb is an empty husk.

MA: What a thing to say!

JULIE: Where's Rog gone? He said he'd stand watch.

PA: Do you know of this boy called Rog?

B.B: I have no knowledge of that name.

PA: Strange he should disappear just as you wander into camp.

MA: I'm sure there's a perfectly good explanation Pa. He'll have been caught short, prob'ly

PA: What do you want, Blind Bastard?

B.B: I asked if I might call upon you again - so here I am calling in for some vegetarian hospitality.

MA: Get some root, Julie. I need to ask Blind Bastard a question.

(Pa sighs, he's not happy with this. But Ma helps Blind Bastard to a chair, and Julie brings a plate of roots and places it in Blind Bastard's waiting hands. He begins to chew straight away.)

B.B: What do you care to know? *I am the eyes of the world.*

MA: Well... it's to do with my shit.

PA: Ma, I don't think...

MA: Please Pa; let me ask him? He might know somethin' we don't.

(Pause.)

MA: I have been shittin' different colors.

B.B: What colors?

MA: Pink, blue, orange... and *yellow*.

B.B: Yellow?

MA: *(Fearful)* Yes... what does it mean?

(Blind Bastard chews for a while on the root as he considers. Eventually...)

B.B: You are chosen.

MA: *Chosen?*

B.B: You have a sign from God.

MA: *I knew it!* What is the sign?

B.B: Your ass is a rainbow.

MA: Oh how wonderful!

PA: Buncha crap!

B.B: Do not doubt, Pa. Our earth received its first punishment millions of years ago when Christ sent an enormous flood to drown mankind. Only Jonah and his family survived; aboard a great ship called The Ark Royal. When the terrible oceans receded and land appeared again, The Lord sent a rainbow - his promise that the world would begin again.

PA: Rainbows are usually in the sky, not stuck up someone's ass.

B.B: The ways of The Lord are strange.

MA: My bottom is holy!

B.B: You are blessed, indeed.

MA: Ooh what a relief! I thought it was somethin' like the whales.

B.B: The whales?

MA: Yellow shit.

B.B: What do you mean?

MA: The whale's shit was yellow.

B.B: Was it?

(Pause.)

PA: That's what you led us to believe, *Holy Man.*

(An uncomfortable pause as Blind Bastard wonders if the game is up. Suddenly he stands, dramatically.)

B.B: *Christ bless this holy woman, whose ass is a testament to your love and forgiveness!!*

PA: *(Plainly)* Take your root an' leave.

B.B: Forgive me: my brain is foggy, clouded by the weight of years - the whale's shit had skipped my mind. Their faeces was indeed yellow and wondrous to behold...

PA: I've had enough of your religious claptrap! Now fuck off while you can still walk! An' don't bother my family again.

B.B: Please point me Eastwards?

(Pa points him eastwards.)

B.B: I have visions...

PA: *Fuck... off!*

B.B: *(Exiting)* This world is cankered to the core - *(Screams)* The end is nigh!!

(Blind Bastard exits. Pause.)

MA: I thought he really was a Holy Man.

PA: Just a hungry scrounger; can't blame him really.

JULIE: He said I have a baby inside me.

PA: You haven't, girl.

JULIE: I might have.

MA: He shouldn't raise people's expectations like that. We all live in hope, *but to tell such awful lies!*

PA: There is no hope, Ma. You can see that - we're on our way out, the whole sorry planet is. S' no good clingin' to some crazy belief; it ain't gonna help... I don't know if it was the whales or the cars or the chemicals that did it; but here we are anyway - the last remnants of a wonderful adventure.

MA: There's still hope, Pa.

PA: No, there's just us and the end, an' that will have to do.

MA: *(Tearful)* *Oh God!* I am so weary an' tired an' sick of scrapin' a life from this dry bone of a world! I'm sick of diggin' for roots an' boilin' bark an' grass, wonderin' if it's all goin' to run out; wonderin' if there's food over the next horizon!

PA: One day there won't be.

MA: What happens then?

(Pause.)

PA: *(Smiles)* You're lovely, y' know. You're worth livin' for.

MA: *(Smiles)* Yeah, life's not so bad, is it?

(Rog approaches the camp. Pa spots him.)

PA: Here comes the boy -

(Rog enters.)

JULIE: We found some more flowers, Rog.

ROG: Yeah?

PA: Where've you been, boy?

ROG: Thought I saw somebody on the horizon; checked it out. But I was lookin' sunward; my eyes might've been playin' tricks.

PA: You missed our visitor.

ROG: What?

MA: We thought he was a Holy Man.

PA: The one who calls himself Blind Bastard. You sure you never heard of him?

ROG: Certain.

PA: Look boy, I'm growin' fond of you. Please don't let me down, will you? Or my girl.

ROG: No, I won't, Pa. I love Julie an' I want to stay with you.

PA: All right. We're movin' on soon *(slaps Rog's shoulder)* - welcome to the family! I'm gettin' some sleep now. See you later.

MA: I'll join you for a nap, Pa. We haven't slept together for ages.

PA: Oh... all right, Ma. Why not, huh? I'm well tuckered, though.

MA: Oh, just a cuddle.

PA: I can manage that.

(Ma and Pa enter the wagon.)

JULIE: Look at these flowers, Rog. Aren't they beautiful?

ROG: They are, Julie.

JULIE: I'm so happy, Rog. I'm so glad I met you.

ROG: Julie -

JULIE: What?

ROG: I've got to tell you somethin'.

JULIE: What's wrong, Rog? You look funny.

ROG: Please sweetheart, understand what I've got to say...

JULIE: You're not leavin', are you?

ROG: I don't want to.

JULIE: Please Rog; don't leave me! I can't face life without you - you make it all worthwhile.

ROG: Truth is...

JULIE: *Oh please..!*

ROG: I'm one of the cannibals from over the ridge.

(Pause.)

JULIE: Are... are you gonna eat me?

ROG: Of course not. I'd never eat you - I love you.

JULIE: I don't understand.

ROG: I came here to do a scout. Blind Bastard *is* known to us; he told us you had a gun... we didn't know if you had bullets.

JULIE: *You're a cannibal.*

ROG: Not any more, Julie. I'll never touch meat again as long as I live. You've changed everythin'

JULIE: Well stay then, don't go!

ROG: After what I told you?

JULIE: I don't care what you did in the past; it's now that matters.

ROG: You sure?

JULIE: *(Hugging him) I love you, you weird lookin' fucker!*

ROG: *Julie!* Oh Christ, Julie it's such a mess!

JULIE: No it's not. Just stay an' everythin' will be all right.

ROG: It won't... Blind Bastard's off to tell the others I've defected. I'll have to go back and stop them from comin'. They might try an' kill ya.

JULIE: We'll fight them!

ROG: I can't risk you an' your family - I'm too involved.

JULIE: There must be somethin' we can do?

ROG: Maybe.

JULIE: What?

ROG: Well... Blind Bastard wants a deal - he'll keep quiet for the can of peaches.

JULIE: I'll get them!

ROG: Oh Julie, you can't. Pa'll never forgive us.

JULIE: I'm not losin' you now.

(Julie enters the wagon and quickly reappears with the can of peaches.)

JULIE: They're snorin' their heads off. No one'll miss it for a while.

ROG: I can't, Julie...

JULIE: *Take it!* Take it an' come back to me!

(Rog takes the can. They embrace.)

ROG: Okay... once it's done; I'm never gonna let you out of my sight. *(Smiles)* You rescued me. I'll be back an' I'll never go away again... I love you so much!

(They kiss passionately, and then Rog heads out into the desert. Julie watches him go with a look of tender passion.)

JULIE: I love you too you weird lookin' bastard!

ROG: *(Calls)* I'll be back tonight.

JULIE: *(Sighs)* Weird bastard! Weird lookin' bastard!

(Music. Cross fade lights to...)

ACT 2, SCENE 4: THE CANNIBAL'S CAMP

(Late afternoon. Blind Bastard is waiting. Scab is a heap of rags near the burnt out car. Rog enters.)

ROG: Alone?

B.B: The others are huntin'. But your presence will not go unnoticed; Scab is restin' nearby.

ROG: *(Calls)* Scab..! Asleep - he won't know. I ought to slice you open an' rip out your black fuckin' heart.

B.B: Do you have the can?

(Rog hands the can to Blind Bastard.)

ROG: Take it, you selfish old bastard!

B.B: Deal done - your secret is safe. I will tell the others you were killed.

(Heather and Bill enter from foraging and spot Rog before he has time to get away.)

BILL: *Well if it isn't the prodigal fuckin' son!*

HEATHER: Where the fuck have you been?!

ROG: With the veggies.

BILL: We thought you were dead!

HEATHER: I see fuck face has got his goddamn can, at last!

BILL: We safe to go in then?

ROG: No, they've got bullets.

BILL: *Fuck!*

HEATHER: That's shit!

ROG: I'm tellin' you.

HEATHER: How come they let you walk away then?

BILL: Yeah, with their can an' all.

ROG: I stole the can.

HEATHER: Bullshit - you're up to somethin'!

BILL: Little suspicious, Rog. What's goin' on?

B.B: He is a traitor! He has rejected the bonds of his true companions and taken up with this abhorrent bunch of grass-masticatin' malingerers!

(Pause.)

BILL: This true, Rog?

ROG: They *have* got a gun.

HEATHER: *You piece of shit!*

ROG: They're good people.

HEATHER: They're supposed to be a good meal!

ROG: I've fallen in love.

HEATHER: *You fallen in fuckin' what?!*

ROG: I can't believe it myself. I can't explain it; it sort of makes life worthwhile. I have to stay with her.

HEATHER: *Girly-skirted pussy-licker!* There's two of us, Bill. *(Takes out knife)* Go for it-

(She waits for Bill to make a move, but he is rooted to the spot.)

HEATHER: What are you waitin' for?

BILL: He's still a friend.

B.B: It is folly to forgive such treachery - he has betrayed your friendship.

BILL: Shut up, Blind Bastard.

B.B: Revenge is a natural law: The Lord himself punished the Ammalekites and Christ struck Eve the Temptress with his own spare rib...

BILL: I said *shut up!!*

(Pause.)

BILL: Fuck off, Rog.

ROG: Can't help it, man.

HEATHER: We're not lettin' him get away with it?!

ROG: *(Exiting)* Good luck - I'll remember ya.

BILL: Just fuck off.

HEATHER: *Have* they got bullets?

(Rog shrugs and heads back. Somehow Heather knows it's the right thing to do; something has happened between them, but they're not sure what it is.)

B.B: I strongly advise against compassion. He has rejected your faith and betrayed your trust.

BILL: You got your peaches, though.

HEATHER: Yeah, you got the can.

B.B: He was compelled by God to deliver the can to my hands.

HEATHER: *He did a deal* - the blind fuckin' prick blackmailed him!

BILL: *(Taking the can from Blind Bastard)* I'll take that.

B.B: *(Screams in panic)* NOOO!! NOOO!! The fruit is meant for my lips only!!

(Bill throws the can to Heather.)

BILL: Use your knife, Heather - slice the top off.

B.B: *The can is mine!!*

(Heather quickly takes off the lid, fishes out a peach slice and pops it in her mouth.)

HEATHER: *Fuckin' hell!*

BILL: What's it like?

HEATHER: Try one –

(Bill takes one and pops it in his mouth. His expression quickly changes.)

BILL: *Christ, they're beautiful!*

B.B: *They are mine!!*

(Heather and Bill proceed to share the peach slices, eating voraciously.)

HEATHER: I've never tasted anythin' like it!

B.B: I command you in God's name to hand me that holy fruit!!

BILL: *(Ignores him)* Where has it all gone? The earth must've been full of stuff like this.

B.B: *(Pleading)* Give me some, please! At least let me taste - I beg you?

HEATHER: These are too good for your shit-hole of a mouth.

B.B: *Please?!*

BILL: I have never tasted anythin' so good!

HEATHER: They seem to burst in your mouth - all sticky an' sweet.

B.B: Christ will inflict your flesh with grotesque cancers!

BILL: *(Taunting him)* Thanks Blind Bastard, they're delicious!

B.B: May you rot from the inside until your very skin erupts, cracks and pours out the pulp of your flesh!

HEATHER: *(Drinking the juice)* Mm, fuckin' mmm! *(Passes the can to Bill)* Take a swig of this, Bill -

BILL: *(Swigs)* Oh God, it's so good! I'll save a drop for Scab.

B.B: I will pray that you suffer lingerin' deaths! I will beg the devil and his thousand hordes to burn your souls for eternity!

BILL: Get lost!

HEATHER: Let's kill him!

BILL: No, just boot him out.

HEATHER: *Oh, not again!*

B.B: *(Exiting)* Beelzebub, the Terminator and all hell's legions will tear your limbs asunder, perpetually!

HEATHER: We're not lettin' another meal walk away?!

BILL: It's unlucky, Heather.

(Heather kicks Blind Bastard off stage.)

HEATHER: Get the fuck out of my life, you walkin' corpse!

B.B: *Aagghhrr!* You assault the Lord's vassal!

HEATHER: No, I'm just assaultin' your skinny ass with my boot!

B.B: *Aagghhrr!* Skank-bitch!

HEATHER: *(Final kick)* Get fucked, you fuckin' fucker!

(Heather stands at the edge of the stage exit as Blind Bastard's voice recedes into the distance.)

B.B: The peaches were meant for *my* lips - the sweet golden treasure of the earth's last spring..!

(Blind Bastard has gone. Heather returns to Bill - they both take one last peach slice and pop it in their mouths. Heather sighs.)

BILL: All gone.

(Bill stares at Heather, he wipes his finger around the rim of the can and holds it out to Heather's lips. She instinctively steps back, and then timidly leans forward and licks his finger.)

HEATHER: Yeah... all gone.

(They look at each other with a mixture of wonder and confusion. For a moment it looks as if Bill might try and kiss her. This is one step too far for her; she shakes herself back to reality.)

HEATHER: Fuckin' Rog, eh? *Fuckin' girly-skirted pussy-licker!*

BILL: Yeah - what a fuckin' pussy-licker!

(Bill looks in the can and smiles.)

BILL: There's some juice left for Scab.

(Bill kneels over Scab.)

BILL: Hey Scab; got somethin' nice, man. Try this - this'll make you feel better...

(Bill uncovers Scab.)

BILL: Scab..? *Oh no! (Begins to cry)* Oh no, poor fucker!

HEATHER: *(Coming over)* What's wrong with you?

BILL: Scab's dead.

HEATHER: 'Bout fuckin' time!

BILL: Poor fucker. He was in a hella lotta pain.

HEATHER: He *was* a pain. Good goddamn riddance, I say.

BILL: For God sake, Heather; didn't you feel anythin' for him?

HEATHER: Yeah - hunger.

BILL: I don't think we should eat him.

HEATHER: *You what?!* This one isn't even alive!

BILL: He didn't want to be eaten. He wanted to be buried.

HEATHER: Bury a good meal? You can go an' fuck yourself!

BILL: I don't think I could eat him.

HEATHER: You wet-assed dipshit! I hate all this pissy sentimentalism! If you want to survive this struggle, you can't afford to start carin' for people.

BILL: Don't you care for anyone?

HEATHER: Yeah - myself.

BILL: Oh eat him, who gives a fuck?!

HEATHER: Yeah - who does?

(Heather uncovers Scab.)

HEATHER: Fuckin' hell - *what a mess!*

BILL: How's your appetite now?

HEATHER: He's covered in fuckin' puss!

BILL: Bit inconsiderate of him.

HEATHER: The bastard! I can't eat that shit - it's all fuckin' disease.

BILL: He wept like a baby last night; like a little baby. His whole body shook with the pain... He kept askin' me if I loved him.

HEATHER: *You what?!*

BILL: He wanted to know I love him.

HEATHER: *You make my heart bleed an' my eyes pump piss!*

BILL: Christ Heather, we've got to care for each other; we've forgot how to love. Rog was right - love makes life worthwhile.

HEATHER: Love won't keep you alive piss-ball. It's hate that keeps you tickin'. Hate that feeds you an' keeps your blood flowin'

BILL: Haven't you ever cared for anyone? What about your family, what about your mother?

HEATHER: My mother baked my little brother when I was eight years old. He was coughin' up blood, but she couldn't wait for him to croak - she caved his tiny head in with a rock. You know what? We all ate the sorry little fucker. You know what? He tasted good; sweetest meat I ever knew. So don't you talk to me about love an' carin', 'cause I ain't never known it an' neither have you, you fuckin' hypocrite!

(Pause.)

BILL: I hope you die before me, because I want to cut off your tits an' roast them over a fuckin' big fire!

HEATHER: *(Grins) That's more like it!*

(Heather turns Scab over to examine the state of his meat.)

HEATHER: What's he like at the back? Anythin' worth salvagin'?

BILL: Don't think it reached his ass.

HEATHER: One buttock each, huh?

BILL: I'll see if I can get a fire goin'.

HEATHER: There's some wood left from last night. I'll go an' get it.

(Heather exits. Bill hates himself for it, but he knows he is going to eat his old friend. Bill touches Scab's face.)

BILL: Sorry Scab... Hey, you should've tasted those peaches, man; you'd have loved them... The world must've been an incredible place at one time, Scab... incredible.

(Pause.)

BILL: I'll bury what's left, ol' friend, promise.

(Music. Cross fade lights to...)

ACT 2, SCENE 5: THE FAMILY'S CAMP

(Early evening. Ma, Pa and Julie are sitting together outside the wagon. Julie is crying.)

PA: It's no good cryin', girl. It ain't gonna make any difference.

JULIE: He's changed Pa, he really has.

PA: You don't just stop bein' a cannibal.

MA: Your Pa's right, Julie. I would never feel safe again. *We could all have been murdered in our beds!*

JULIE: He wouldn't, I know it!

PA: I can't believe you gave him the can.

JULIE: I had to!

PA: Couldn't you see he was stringin' you along?

JULIE: I don't think he was.

MA: Fooled twice we have since we've been here!

PA: Yeah, well no more.

MA: You said it was funny he disappeared when the phoney prophet came along.

PA: In cahoots.

JULIE: Pa... I really think he was tellin' the truth.

PA: Savin' that can, we was.

MA: Very valuable.

PA: I'll never trust a soul again.

MA: It's a sad world.

JULIE: It's not...

(Pa suddenly leaps to his feet.)

PA: Christ, he's comin'! I can see him just over that rise in the ground.

JULIE: *(Delighted)* I told you he'd come back!

PA: Gun, girl -

JULIE: *No Pa!*

PA: Gun, Ma -

(Ma passes Pa his gun.)

JULIE: He wouldn't come back if he didn't mean it. He's a veggie now - he's one of us.

PA: We can never trust him again. He conned you out of the peaches, an' don't forget what he came here to do - *he told you.*

JULIE: He confessed it because he loves me.

PA: You silly girl; he was manipulatin' you, takin' you into his confidence.

MA: Trust your Pa, Julie. He knows best.

JULIE: I love him..!

MA: He was suspicious of the prophet, quite rightly.

JULIE: I'll kill myself.

PA: No you won't.

JULIE: I can't live without him.

PA: You'll have to.

MA: It's a cruel world, Julie; you're gonna to have to get used to it.

PA: Here he is - the great pretender!

(Rog enters. Pa raises his gun.)

ROG: Pa... what's the gun for?

JULIE: He made me tell him, Rog; when you'd gone an' he found the can was missin'.

PA: What happened to the peaches?

ROG: I can explain...

PA: You're a cannibal, ain't ya?

ROG: Not anymore.

PA: That can belonged to my father.

ROG: I had to do a deal. Maybe it was a mistake...

PA: Where are your friends?

ROG: There's only a couple left.

PA: *Liar!* Why did you take the can?

ROG: I did it for Julie. I want to stay with her.

PA: No way, cannibal!

ROG: I've changed.

PA: You're finished, boy.

ROG: Please don't kill me.

PA: I have to, boy. You've left me no choice.

JULIE: *No Pa!*

PA: I can't listen this time, girl. Can't take the risk.

ROG: *(With realization)* You got bullets, then?

PA: *(Nods)* Sorry.

(Pa shoots him. Rog's guts explode. He falls to his knees, covered in blood.)

ROG: *Oh shit! Oh fuckin' shit..! Oh fuckin' shit!*

(Julie runs to Rog and embraces him.)

JULIE: *Rog!*

ROG: *Shit Julie... fuckin' shit!*

(Rog dies in Julie's arms. Pause.)

MA: Why did he say shit?

JULIE: *(Crying)* Oh Pa, you've killed him!

PA: I'm sorry, girl. It's all for the best.

JULIE: Rog... oh Rog! *I loved him, Ma!*

MA: I know you did, Julie. But your Pa was right - he fooled us all.

(Pa is much affected by his deed.)

PA: *(Weeping)* Look at that! Look at that bloody mess! Goddamn peaches!

JULIE: He loved me... he gave me a flower, an' it rained.

MA: I wonder what they tasted like?

PA: Who cares?

(Music as the lights fade to blackout.)

ACT 2, SCENE 6: THE FAMILY'S CAMP

(Lights up on the family's camp. Late morning a few days later. Ma and Pa are sitting around a fire. Something is cooking in the ashes.)

PA: We'll have to move out first thing tonight. There's a good moon just now; keep out of the daylight - it's definitely gettin' hotter.

MA: I'm findin' it very difficult to breathe properly.

PA: S' your asthma.

MA: There's not enough air.

PA: Yeah, got me a poundin' headache too. How's your shit been today?

MA: Brown.

PA: *(Pleased)* Same as mine!

MA: Must be normal then, huh?

PA: Must be.

(Julie enters from the wagon.)

PA: How are you feelin' now, girl?

MA: She's better now, Pa. All cried out, ain't you?

JULIE: I'm pregnant.

PA: No girl, you're not. I keep tellin' you - it's not possible.

JULIE: Rog planted his seed inside me an' it's growin' into somethin' beautiful.

MA: You're not pregnant, Julie - honestly. Nobody will ever be pregnant again. The world is too messed up.

JULIE: The world is startin' up again.

PA: Resolve, girl: face the truth an' bite the bullet.

JULIE: There's a baby inside me, crawlin' around.

MA: There isn't a baby, there's nothin'. It's not possible, Julie.

JULIE: It is. I've got a little tiny baby inside me, singin' - I can hear it.

(Pa fishes some meat from the fire: an anklebone with a foot attached. He offers it to Julie.)

PA: Here - have a piece of leg.

(Pause and then Julie takes it.)

JULIE: I'll eat it for the baby's sake.

PA: Good girl.

(Julie wanders off a few paces and settles down on her own.)

JULIE: *(Talking to her stomach)* It's your daddy, baby. It's your lovely daddy comin' down inside me to feed you. He'll make you strong an' special. An' when you come out we're gonna pick flowers together.

(Julie begins to eat the leg. Ma and Pa watch, protectively.)

MA: Wish she'd get over these fantasies.

PA: She'll be all right, Ma.

MA: I hope so.

PA: At least she's keepin' her food down now.

MA: Yeah.

(Music. Cross fade lights to...)

ACT 2, SCENE 7: THE CANNIBAL'S CAMP

(Late afternoon, the same day. Bill is alone, poking the embers of a dead fire. Heather enters carrying a sack.)

HEATHER: Hello thumb dick!

BILL: Hello fuck face.

HEATHER: You still fuckin' mopin'?

BILL: S'pose so.

HEATHER: You're a prick!

BILL: Yeah I know.

HEATHER: Scab was a prick, too, an' Rog.

BILL: Miss 'em though.

HEATHER: Bet you wouldn't miss me.

BILL: Of course I would. You're the only person I know.

(Pause.)

BILL: What you got in the sack?

(Heather pulls out Blind Bastard's head.)

HEATHER: *(Imitating his voice)* "I am the eyes of the world!"

BILL: *Oh fuck,* you've killed Blind Bastard!

HEATHER: Rest of him's cut into strips, dryin' in the sun.

BILL: *There'll be bad luck!*

HEATHER: Yeah? That'll make a change.

BILL: S'pose I expected it sooner or later. No way was you gonna let him live much longer.

HEATHER: *(Laughs)* I killed him ever so slow - you should've heard him fuckin' squeal!

BILL: Flesh for flesh, huh?

HEATHER: *(Smiles)* Yeah - *flesh for flesh!*

BILL: What you gonna do with the head? Boil it?

HEATHER: Don't think so. I've been down to the brook.

BILL: Yeah?

HEATHER: It isn't there.

BILL: *What?!*

HEATHER: Dried up.

BILL: Christ, we're dead!

HEATHER: We'll have to move on tonight.

BILL: What's the point? We're fucked! You've brought a curse down on us.

HEATHER: I killed Blind Bastard *after* I went for water; reckoned we'd need some food for the journey.

(Pause. Bill looks at Heather as if for the first time and Heather suddenly feels uncomfortable.)

BILL: Give me a kiss, Heather?

HEATHER: *Give you a fuckin' what?!*

BILL: Come on - give me a kiss. I want to know what it feels like.

HEATHER: You can go an' fuck yourself!

BILL: Please Heather; kiss me. I might not get another chance.

(Pause. Heather is completely stumped, but Rog's appearance has been working away at them; she decides to give it a go. She drops the sack and stands in front of Bill.)

HEATHER: I ain't never done this before.

(They kiss. Tentatively at first, then they begin to enjoy it. After a few tender moments, they embrace, surprised and bewildered and Heather steps away.)

BILL: What do you think?

HEATHER: It's all right.

BILL: Stay with me, Heather.

HEATHER: We'll go together, Bill.

BILL: No, I'm not goin'.

HEATHER: You've got to - we'll die.

BILL: How far do you think we'll get without water?

(The truth hits Heather like a sledgehammer - they are going to die and there is nothing they can do about it. Her lips tremble as she stares at Bill. Bill stares back, sadly, and then a thin trace of a smile creases his face as he extends a hand to her. For the first time in her life Heather begins to cry - she sobs like a baby as Bill embraces her and pulls her tight.)

HEATHER: We've got to try.

BILL: Why?

(Pause. They kiss again.)

HEATHER: *(Smiles tearfully)* Your breath stinks, Bill.

BILL: *(Smiles back)* Yours too, you lesbian.

(They kiss again. Suddenly there is a low rumble which quickly grows in intensity, the stricken orange sky is now a frightening blood red - they both know its the end, and so they cling desperately to each other in terror. The rumbling is now an almost unbearable thunder, and stuff blows all around the set as the very air they breathe is quickly dissolving as the Earth's atmosphere disappears. Its plain to see they are choking for breath as they sink to the ground still clinging to each other. The blood red light flickers between black and red, and the pain on their faces is frighteningly clear as they gasp their last breath, falling down together in a final deadly embrace; a last twitch of limbs signifying their death. The rumbling ends and the stage is plunged into an eerie blackness as the relentless solar wind moans and the sky backdrop is peppered with stars and constellations sparkling like diamonds against the deep black of Earth's eternal night.)

END OF PLAY.
.

NOTES

NOTES